Joanna Hall

THE GI WALKING DIET

LOSE 10LBS AND 10 YEARS IN 6 WEEKS

HARPER
thorsons

By the same author:

The 24 Hour Diet
The Step Counter Fitness Diet
No Carbs After 5pm Diet
Drop a Size for Life
Drop a Size Calorie and Carb Counter
Drop a Size in 2 Weeks Flat

HarperThorsons
An Imprint of HarperCollins*Publishers*
77–85 Fulham Palace Road
Hammersmith, London W6 8JB

The website address is: www.thorsonselement.com

and *HarperThorsons* are trademarks of
HarperCollins*Publishers* Limited

Published by HarperThorsons 2006

10 9 8 7 6 5 4 3 2 1

Joanna Hall's website address is www.joannahall.com

Photography by Dan Welldon, www.danwelldon.com

A catalogue record for this book is
available from the British Library

ISBN-13 978-0-00-722144-8
ISBN-10 0-00-722144-4

Printed in Great Britain by
Martins the Printers Ltd, Berwick upon Tweed

Contents

Introduction: Active Ageing – One Foot in the Future

Ageing isn't really ageing – it's inactivity that's the problem

As we progress through life, we may find it more challenging to be as active as we once were. The ageing process imposes changes upon our bodies that can gradually reduce our capabilities, but this can be compounded by lack of physical activity. There are many reasons for being inactive. Often, life seems to get in the way as we spend time focusing on careers, bringing up a family or caring for elderly relatives. We may be so busy that we feel guilty about taking time out for ourselves. Whatever the reasons, you may find your middle has got thicker and you're not feeling quite the way you'd like to at this stage in your life.

Sedentary lifestyles contribute to a number of physical complaints that start to creep in as we get older. Suffering from – or a fear of suffering from – arthritis, diabetes, osteoporosis, creaky knees or a troublesome back can all be potential barriers to getting us moving. The sad truth is that by not taking an active role in your body's ageing, you are accelerating the process of decay. Yet there is a viable alternative that can make you feel better, look better and lose that middle-age spread.

How Active are You?

Asking people to define their level of activity is often a sensitive issue. In my experience of working with clients, I have found that many of us tend to over-estimate how active we are. This is not because we are lazy, though some of us by our own admission do prefer to curl up with a good book. To me, the confusion comes from the different ways we can define being active.

Ask anyone about their day and they usually reply that they are tired because they have been very busy and active. We naturally associate tiredness with a physically active day. When you probe a bit deeper, however, you often find that their day has not been physically active – it has been active in quite a different way. You can, in fact, be *geographically* or *mentally* active.

Here's the scenario for a geographically active day. You wake up and think about the things that have to be done. You need to drop clothes off at the dry cleaners, pick up dog food for Fido, get to work, get across town for a lunch meeting, get back to the office to finish a report, grab something for dinner at the supermarket, get home, unload the car, cook dinner, get things ready for tomorrow. It gets to 8pm. You are tired. You have had a busy day and you've been all over town but you have not moved your body much – the car has moved, the train has moved but in reality your body has not really moved that much. You have been geographically active but not physically active.

Here's the scenario for a mentally active day. You wake up in the morning, having been up half the night thinking about all the things you need to do. The monthly report needs to be completed before 10am, and the sales director wants figures by 11am. You've got a dinner party to plan for Saturday night, and you need to do the online shop by midday to get the home delivery service to deliver by 5pm on Friday. Your tax return is late so you need to get on with it. You also need to speak to the family about the arrangements for Christmas or that special occasion. It gets to 8pm. You are tired. You have had a busy day. Your brain has been all over the place – but you have not moved your body much. You have been mentally active but not physically active.

Our days will always be geographically active and mentally active but we have to encourage ourselves to be more physically active, and this is where this book comes in.

Time for Action

At this stage in your life, you may find you have more time for yourself than before. Your children may have left home. You may be retired or working part-time. This could be a real opportunity for you to make time to get active.

I have designed the GI Walking Diet to be realistic and achievable for every-one. What one person might find achievable could be difficult for someone else. That's why you will find a variety of programmes that actively assist and guide you to improve your health and fitness and achieve sustainable weight loss. While the overall plan guides you to walk your way to fitness, weight loss and health improvements in just six weeks, your progress starts with small steps that are achievable for just about everyone.

In Chapter 1 we'll look at the physical changes that occur as we get older. Chapter 2 tells you all about the emotional side of ageing. Chapter 3 explains how taking small steps can bring about big changes to your lifestyle. In Chapter 4 you'll find out about the GI Walking Diet, why it's achievable and the huge impact it can have on your health. In Chapter 5 we'll address exactly where you are now and how you can get ready for your six-week plan. In Chapters 6 and 7, the plan is clearly laid out. All the exercises are described and illustrated so they are easy to follow, and the week-by-week guide gives you both a structure and a flexible approach to success, guiding you to achievable results, whatever your ability. Getting in shape and losing weight doesn't mean missing out on great food, and in Chapter 8 you'll find delicious recipes that easily fall in with the GI style of eating you can enjoy on your way better health.

> Having good intentions about starting a diet and exercise plan is one thing – knowing *where* to start can be a minefield. My specially-designed 'at a glance guides' in Chapter 6 will help you get going. You can use them as starting points or as handy references as you progress with the programme.

Weight loss *can* be a significant motivator for us to change our habits, get a grip and make a difference. As we get older, however, it can seem more difficult to lose weight. We may also become more accepting of our expanding waistlines. Many people mistakenly believe that the only way to improve their health is to lose large amounts of weight and spend lots of time exercising, which just seems like too much effort. For many, a rotund, cuddly figure can become an acceptable part of later life.

But stop right there! You can make a significant difference to your health without too much hard work. You don't have to lose large amounts of weight to experience real health benefits. In fact, a weight loss of just 5–10 per cent provides major health benefits. So, if you weigh 16 stone (100kg), a drop of between 8lb (3kg) to 1 stone 2lb (7kg) can make a major difference. Accepting this fact makes the whole process much more realistic and achievable.

So the time has come to take action. No more excuses. Stop kidding yourself – or your middle-age spread and muscle stiffness are here to stay. Start taking small steps to create big changes to your health, your weight, your fitness, your energy and your self-esteem. If you're ready, I'll show you how.

I

Dealing Positively with Ageing

Fitness for a young person is an option –
for an older person it's imperative

1 Physical Changes

"I don't feel old. I don't feel anything till noon.
Then it's time for my nap." *Bob Hope*

How Old Do You Feel?

So you woke up this morning, got out of bed and looked in the mirror – what did you think of the person staring back at you? You may be a parent, a grandparent, a lover, a wife, a husband, a son, a daughter. But as you reflect on yourself and your current stage in life, how do you actually feel about yourself and how do you see your body?

Do you think of yourself as:
- Young
- Young at heart
- Youthful
- Fit
- Active

- Agile
- Sexy
- Darn good for my age
- Not bad considering …
- Middle-aged
- A bit baggy and saggy
- Age is creeping up on me fast!
- My body needs an overhaul
- Old
- Wanting a new body
- Elderly
- My memory is going fast
- Decrepit

In my research for this book, I interviewed over a thousand men and women aged over 50. I asked them about their eating and activity habits, for their views on their bodies and their attitudes to this phase of their lives. Their thoughts, views, needs and wants – coupled with the exciting new advances being made in research – have directly shaped this book.

So what did my research tell me?
- 83 per cent thought that their body needed an overhaul
- 39 per cent considered themselves young at heart
- 77 per cent described themselves as a bit baggy and saggy
- 51 per cent considered themselves old
- Over 85 per cent of respondents wanted to address weight loss and middle-age spread and improve their health
- Sadly, less than 1 per cent considered themselves sexy

Changing Your Attitudes and Habits

You may feel daunted by the physical changes you are experiencing as you grow older. However, the exciting thing about this phase is that you now have the ability – more than at any other time in your life – to make a significant impact on your health. You also have more to gain from your efforts than at any other time.

Active ageing is as much about attitude as it is about action. Your children may have flown the nest; you may have retired; you may have more time on your hands – and this is the time for you. It's an age of choice without limitations, a time of joy with few constraints. While some of us may still have some demands on our time, this does not detract from the fact that this stage in your life represents the best window of opportunity for your physical body.

And you know what? The only things that may be stopping you from taking action are your attitude and deep-rooted habits. Attitudes and habits can be difficult to change – after all, you may have been nurturing them for decades.

I've designed all the plans in this book so you can grab and make the most of this window of opportunity. They not only deliver results but also help you nurture new, healthier habits and attitudes without feeling you have to give up the life you enjoy. By making small changes on a regular, consistent basis, you can lose weight, feel fitter, enjoy more energy and even sleep better. These small steps together mean big changes for you and your body.

So don't you dare think you've left it too late. It's never too late. The time has come to open the window of opportunity, stop being complacent about this phase of your life, take a deep breath and go for it.

One Step at a Time

When you first look at the plan you may feel a little daunted about what you have to do. The plan has been designed to be simple and easy to follow. You'll see that you get to choose whether to start the walking plan at an 'entry' or 'advanced' level, depending on your current fitness level (see Chapter 4).

I'd be the first to acknowledge, however, that life can be busy and throw us different challenges. Family commitments, work and health issues can all make it seem difficult to find time to exercise. While I wouldn't encourage you to use these busy times as excuses, I'd far rather you did something than wait for the 'perfect' time to start. In my experience, the perfect time rarely comes, and since this stage of your life is your greatest window of opportunity, this may be the perfect time to approach your plan in a phased way. For example, you may choose to follow the flexibility plan for the first six weeks, then the strength programme for weeks six to twelve, and finally the walking plan for weeks twelve to eighteen. A phased approach such as this will get you on the road to success. You'll feel healthier and more in control, although your weight loss may be a little slower than if you were following the complete plan.

Timetable for a Phased Approach to the GI Walking Diet

You start with:	Why:
Flexibility Plan	You are completely new to exercise. You may be recovering from an operation or getting back on the road to full health.
Strength Plan	You like the idea of feeling more toned. You may have limited heart and lung stamina, so the strength plan is more attractive as an easy exercise starter, plus you'll be building up your leg strength ready for your walking programme.
Walking Plan	You want to see some weight come off and enjoy more aerobic activity.
Flexibility and Strength Plans	You may feel unable to commit to the walking plan – or you may prefer to ease in to the plan gently.

Benefits:	Weeks
You'll reconnect with your body, experience big improvements in your posture, balance and body confidence, plus it will easily slot into your day without feeling too taxing physically or time wise.	Weeks 1–6
You'll get more muscle tone. Your body will look better and you'll feel more physically confident in a variety of ways – as your body will be able to complete tasks which may previously have felt more challenging.	Weeks 6–12
Selecting the entry or advanced plan puts you in control of your efforts, allowing you to progress at the right pace for you. Combining the walking plan with the eating plan will help you see the pounds drop off and the inches fall away.	Weeks 12–18
This is a great combination for boosting your body confidence. These two plans complement each other well – fast-tracking you on the road to success.	Weeks 1–6

How the Body Ages

Nobody wants their body to age, but the great news is that you can slow down the rate of ageing. In fact, ageing can a positive experience, not the negative one many of us feel and dread.

In physical terms, the ageing process results in a gradual loss of coordination, flexibility, strength, power and endurance. These physiological changes can have a significant impact on our emotions, our ability to lead independent lives and our energy and self-esteem.

Whether you like it or not, your body will go through a number of changes as it ages. How these changes affect you is partly dependent on your genes, diet, and how physically active you have been through your life. Think about how your parents or siblings have aged and you'll have a good indication of how your body is affected by your genes. The geneticist Claude Bouchard believes that genes determine 60 to 80 per cent of the body's rate of physical change; other factors, such as diet and the amount and type of physical activity we take, can change our bodies by 20 to 40 per cent.

Fortunately, evidence suggests that your physical activity levels *after* the age of 35 can have a more significant effect on how you age than the amount of exercise taken in earlier years. Although you may not be able to reverse declines in physical function, they can be slowed down. Understanding what is happening to your body can help you appreciate how your diet and activity levels can positively impact upon your weight, energy, posture and, most importantly, how you look and feel about yourself.

A fit man at 70 is the same as an unfit man at 40.

Much of the deterioration attributed to ageing is now linked to physical inactivity. Our goal is to push back frailty to a very small part of life experience. Or, as the philosopher Ashley Montagne has urged, 'To die young as late in life as possible.'

You can do this without spending masses of time exercising, waving goodbye to your existing lifestyle or surviving on a diet of bizarre foods. And you can do this in just six weeks.

Ageing and Physical Ability

Strength, power, endurance and flexibility are terms we often hear, but understanding exactly what they mean will help you appreciate your own body's needs, allowing you to tailor the six-week plan to your needs.

Strength and Power

Muscular strength refers to the maximum force that can be exerted by a muscle group. You may be more familiar with strength referring to the maximum weight or load that can be lifted once. Power refers to the greatest amount of force that can be exerted, and requires both strength and speed of movement. This may all sound rather technical, but in real terms the impact of these capacities on your body can be far-reaching. Muscle strength declines significantly with advancing age, which results in a decreased ability to perform many daily tasks. Activities such as lifting heavy shopping bags can become difficult. Your grandchild may need to be handed to you rather than you being able to lift them directly from the floor. Even getting out of a low chair can pose a problem, perhaps requiring a few momentum-gathering rocks backwards and forwards to get you up. Later in life, both strength and power are important for balance and reducing the risk of falling.

Endurance

Endurance, often referred to as stamina, is a muscle's ability to keep going. All muscles need endurance – the muscles of your legs need it to keep walking, for example – but one of the most important muscles is the heart. The endurance of your heart is vital to your wellbeing, and it's often referred to as your 'huff and puff'. Having poor endurance means that it can be hard work running after a bus, train or walking briskly up a hill. Climbing a flight of stairs can leave you feeling uncomfortable and breathless. If you have young grand-children, you'll know how much energy and endurance they have and how you need to be able to keep up with them!

Flexibility and Mobility

Flexibility refers to the range of motion at a particular joint, while mobility refers to the ability to take your joints through this range. Flexibility and mobil-ity are determined by the elasticity of the connective tissue, as well as the specific length of individual ligaments and tendons. As we age, the connective tissue becomes less elastic. The special lubricating synovial fluid – found inside certain joints such as the hip, knee and shoulder – becomes less mobile and runny. This makes joints feel stiff and perhaps a bit 'clicky', limiting the range of motion we may be able to take them through. This can make it difficult to unzip a back-fastening piece of clothing, to reach up for something on a top shelf or to bend down to pick something up. Maybe even getting your leg up and over the bath can be a bit of a challenge, requiring you to hold on to some-thing for support. Or perhaps you find when you need to turn to see something you have to turn your whole body around, instead of just being able to rotate at your waist.

The bottom line is that maintaining your level of physical capacity in terms of strength, endurance and flexibility is very important for continued independence. Power, strength and flexibility are all closely related, and improving one of these will have a knock-on effect on the others. The GI Walking Diet enables you to improve all these abilities in a simple, effective and easy-to-follow way.

Physiological Effects of Ageing

Resting Metabolic Rate

Your resting metabolic rate (RMR) is the amount of calories your body requires just to live. It's determined by your weight and the amount of muscle and body fat you have. As we age, RMR tends to decline. This is partly due to decreased muscle mass. It's also affected by changes to your nervous system, specifically the sympathetic nervous system (SNS), slowing the response time between brain messages and muscle movement. Resting metabolic rate is what most people mean when they say 'basal metabolic rate' (BMR). These two terms are used interchangeably, although they are not technically the same.

As part of the normal ageing process, most body organs decrease in functional capacity, resulting in a 2 per cent decline in BMR each decade. However, if physical activity also declines, BMR will decrease more quickly, and there will be a greater increase in fat mass. This means that, over time, your metabolic rate slows down, and weight gain will occur unless you decrease the amount of calories you consume and increase your level of physical activity. Your metabolic rate may also decrease as the cardiovascular, gastrointestinal and respiratory systems slow down with age, which can influence digestion, absorption and nutrition needs.

What This Means to You

The biggest impact of a reduced RMR is that you will find it more difficult to maintain a healthy weight, and you may experience weight gain.

What You Can Do

Experts are divided on how much weight gain is a product of the natural ageing process and how much is attributable to other factors, such as decreased energy expenditure through physical activity. But one thing's certain: decreased physical activity results in less muscle mass, which in turn impacts upon your RMR or the rate at which the body burns calories. But it doesn't have to be like this …

Action Worth Investing In

By following the six-week plan, specifically the walking and strength programme, you can feel confident that you will lose weight.

VO$_2$ MAX

Most researchers who have evaluated the effects of ageing on the stamina of the heart and lungs have focused on 'maximal aerobic fitness' or VO$_2$ MAX. This refers to the body's maximum ability to take in oxygen, transport it around the body in the blood and use it to burn fuel in the muscles. This is considered to be the single best indicator of the changes that occur in the body with ageing. After 25 years of age, VO$_2$ MAX normally declines at a rate of 8 to 10 per cent per decade for both men and women. Approximately half of this decrease has been related to people exercising less and gaining weight as they age.

We all tend to have different VO$_2$ MAX values. Athletes have very high values, meaning that their bodies are better able to take in oxygen and use it to produce energy. Normal people have more average levels. With age, however, nature takes its toll on all of us and we all experience a decrease in our VO$_2$ MAX.

What This Means to You

A lowering in your VO_2 MAX can cause a decrease in your performance, your everyday 'huff and puff'. Physical tasks that seemed easy now require a little more effort. You may feel out of breath and that you don't have enough energy. But it doesn't have to be like this …

What You Can Do

At any age, if you exercise vigorously and keep lean you can have a much higher VO_2 MAX. Research has shown that athletes aged from 65 to 75 can have the VO_2 MAX of young sedentary adults and are capable of performing at levels once thought physically unattainable.

But we do have to be realistic. Even among older athletes who exercise vigorously throughout their lives, VO_2 MAX will still eventually decline. The important point, however, is that the rate of decline will be much slower. A US study examining former elite long-distance runners over a 22-year period found that regardless of how much they trained, all did eventually lose aerobic fitness; but (and this is a big BUT) the rate of decline may be lessened for up to 20 years if an individual takes regular vigorous endurance exercise.

Action Worth Investing In

You'll find that the six-week walking plan can have a significant impact on your cardiovascular fitness. It will give you more huff and puff and loads more energy. If you combine it with the six-week menu plan, you'll lose 5–10 per cent of your excess weight. Your clothes will fit better and you will look younger.

Oestrogen

For women, oestrogen plays a significant role in controlling calcium absorption and retention in the bones, so when it starts to decline it can have a big impact on the body.

What This Means to You

Without adequate oestrogen, women over the age of 50 are at increased risk of osteoporosis, stress fractures or broken bones. (You can find out more about osteoporosis on page 22.) In addition, research is showing how calcium has a vital role in helping the body burn fat. The exact mechanism is not entirely understood but studies have shown that when people consume inadequate amounts of calcium, the body stores more fat, resulting in weight gain. But it doesn't have to be like this …

What You Can Do

Most experts say that calcium should come from the diet. (For details of good dietary calcium sources, see page 190.) Resistance training is an excellent way for women of all ages to stimulate and maintain bone growth. Hormone replacement therapy, although once considered promising, now appears to have little or no positive effect on bone mass growth.

Action Worth Investing In

Following the six-week menu plan will help boost your calcium intake, while just by completing the six-week strength plan twice a week, you'll experience big improvements in your physical capacity, body tone and strength.

Other Hormones

Many hormones play a significant role in the body. As we age, hormonal changes can affect us in many ways. You will come across a number of them in this book – here is an overview of the most important ones.

- **Human growth hormone:** secreted in much greater amounts in youth to help bones grow. Also helps the body to metabolize fats. Levels tend to diminish with age, which is thought to contribute to decreases in cell membrane composition.

- **Progesterone:** the gestational hormone, which prepares the lining of the uterus for the fertilized egg and maintains pregnancy. Progesterone is a 'precursor' hormone, which can be converted by the body into other steroid hormones. As levels fall, an imbalance occurs between this hormone and the other primary female sex hormone, oestrogen. This is linked with weight gain, decreases in bone density and a possible reduction in sex drive.

- **Testosterone:** the male sex hormone, most commonly known for promoting libido and stimulating sperm production. Also helps protein build muscles, skin and bone, and nourishes all the tissues of the male urinary and reproductive systems. Regulates the production of prostaglandin, which seems to keep prostate growth under control. In both sexes, testosterone levels decrease with age. This has a significant impact on health and wellbeing, contributing to decreases in bone and muscle development as well as reduced virility. Recent evidence has linked low testosterone with Alzheimer's disease.

- **DHEA:** dubbed the 'mother of all hormones' because the body uses it to produce a number of hormones including testosterone, oestrogen and progesterone. DHEA production drops sharply after the age of 25; by the age of 75 we are producing only 10–20 per cent of the DHEA our bodies manufactured at 20, and this has an impact on the other sex hormones.

◆ **Thyroid hormones:** regulate the body's metabolism, temperature and heart rate. If the thyroid isn't functioning at its optimal level, neither are you. Thyroid deficiency is not specifically age-related as woman can be prone to it at all ages, especially during and after pregnancy.

◆ **Insulin:** the main hormone for promoting the transport of glucose rather than fat into muscle cells to be used as energy; also a potent inhibitor of the fat-stimulating hormone HSL. Excess body fat is associated with insulin resistance. Some researchers have suggested that reducing body fat through calorie restriction without under-nutrition may help improve the insulin response, which can reduce risk factors for disease. You can enhance your insulin sensitivity by increasing your intake of the healthy omega-3 fatty acids found in oily fish such as salmon, mackerel and fresh tuna, and in walnuts, flaxseeds and soya products. Vigorous exercise can also improve insulin sensitivity.

◆ **Epinephrine and cortisol:** prepare the body for an instant state of readiness – the classic 'fight or flight' response. Epinephrine is the primary hormone that stimulates lipolysis, the breakdown of fat. Epinephrine binds to the receptors on various cells and can either activate or inhibit HSL, the hormone responsible for fat mobilization. Epinephrine excretion appears not to change with age. Cortisol releases glucose and fatty acids into the bloodstream to provide energy to the muscles. It also has a direct impact on the body's blood sugar levels. If too little cortisol is released, hypoglycaemia (low blood sugar) can develop; if too much cortisol is released, hyperglycaemia (high blood sugar) can develop, which can increase the risk of developing diabetes. When people experience prolonged stress, cortisol levels remain elevated for long periods, and recent research shows that this can lead to weight gain, especially on the belly. Cortisol excretion appears to increase with age.

Intestinal Bacteria

Our intestinal bacteria can play a role in weight gain as we age. Atrophic gastritis is a bacterial infection marked by a decreased ability to produce sufficient amounts of gastric acids. This condition occurs in 24 per cent of people aged 60–69 years, 32 per cent of people aged 70–79 and about 40 per cent of people over the age of 80.

What This Means to You
Low-acidic conditions in the stomach can affect the absorption of nutrients such as folic acid, vitamin B12, calcium, iron and betacarotene.

What You Can Do
If you suffer from atrophic gastritis, you are usually advised to get adequate calories by eating small meals throughout the day or by snacking on nutrient-dense foods. You should avoid nutrient-poor choices such as commercial biscuits and cakes. Medication may also be prescribed for this condition. Speak to your doctor if you feel you may be suffering from intestinal bacteria problems. Symptoms include bloating, discomfort and poor digestion.

Action Worth Investing In
The six-week menu plan and all the recipes are designed to provide you with an optimum nutrition plan that is both enjoyable and easy to adapt to your lifestyle, whether you are entertaining or looking after the family.

Connective Tissue

Ageing brings about stiffening of the connective tissue such as your tendons and ligaments. This leads to a loss of mobility.

What This Means to You

This may make your joints feel stiff, affecting your mobility and ability to react physically and move the way you want. When walking, you may experience an increased postural sway – moving the upper body from side to side –which affects your stride length, gait and balance. When gait and balance are affected, the risk of falling increases. But it doesn't have to be like this …

What You Can Do

Improving your mobility is a simple and highly effective way to improve your range of motion and your quality of movement.

Action Worth Investing In

You'll find your mobility action plan invaluable (see page 146). You can do it every day, and in fewer than 14 days you'll notice a difference in how your body feels; and after three weeks you'll notice a big improvement in how it moves. You'll also find the tips on walking technique helpful for enhancing mobility (see page 63).

Body Stages

> The body is on a journey. Like any journey,
> the ride may not always be smooth.

For women in particular, hormones play a large part in the changes we notice as we get older. However, men also see their bodies changing as they pass through different stages in life.

Peri-menopause

Peri-menopause is defined as the time leading up to menopause. For some women, this can be eight to ten years before the onset of the menopause itself. Marked by a fluctuation of hormones, it is often described as a roller-coaster ride since the decline in hormones is erratic rather than steady.

During peri-menopause, many women experience a range of symptoms, including:

◆ Mood swings
◆ Memory loss
◆ Bone loss
◆ Potential detrimental changes to their cholesterol levels
◆ Hot flushes
◆ Sleep disturbances

At this stage in their lives, women also experience a drop in metabolism, owing to changes in hormones and muscle mass. This means their bodies require fewer calories to perform normal everyday tasks, and slowly this contributes to weight gain. Oestrogen levels become more erratic, waxing and waning, which causes fat to be stored in the abdomen. Consequently, any weight gain is laid down around the middle, and so middle-age spread is born!

Erratic levels of the hormone oestrogen cause fat to be stored around the abdomen – and so middle-age spread is born!

Peri-menopause is a critical period for a woman's health. During this time, healthy habits – like regular exercise, good nutrition and an element of stress management – are vital to prepare for the next stage of your life, and to help you handle the physiological and associated emotional changes being experienced.

How the GI Walking Diet Can Help

Follow the six-week plan and you will make a great investment in your health. The structure of the programme will help you form good habits, while all the tips along the way will show you how these physical investments can fit easily into your lifestyle.

Menopause

Menopause is defined as the 12 months after a woman's final menstrual period, which is usually around the age of 52. Although we tend to think of menopause as a single point in the body's journey, both peri-menopause and menopause are more like peaks and troughs than finite events. After menopause, women lose about 66 per cent of their oestrogen and 50 to 60 per cent of their testosterone. Oestrogen tends to decline at a faster rate than testosterone, and so testosterone can start to have a greater effect on the body. In most cases, body fat is redistributed from the hips to the midriff. This 'shape-shifting' phenomenon compounds the middle-age spread that you may have started to experience during peri-menopause. Blood pressure and cholesterol levels rise. The loss of oestrogen's protective influence on bone tissue leads to decreases in bone mineral density. On average, women lose 2 per cent of bone mass each year during menopause, yet it is possible to lose up to 20 per cent of bone in the five to seven years after menopause.

While all these changes are happening inside the body, women can experience a range of unpleasant symptoms such as:

- Hot flushes
- Memory loss
- Slowed metabolism
- Mood swings
- Sexual difficulties

Some of the physical effects of menopause – weight gain, the 'shape-shifting' scenario and changes in blood pressure and cholesterol – can put women at a higher risk of cardiovascular disease.

How the GI Walking Diet Can Help

The six-week walking plan will be particularly valuable for your health. You don't have to be super fit – just turn to page 124 and you can choose a starting level to suit you. It really is that simple to start walking off your weight.

The Window of Opportunity Years

The 'window of opportunity years' are a time of choice – when you can choose to open the window and experience the benefits of health and fitness. As women move beyond the menopause, and men reach their mid-50s and 60s, normal changes to the body include:

- Decreases in the amount of cardiovascular exercise you can perform
- Slowing of your reaction time
- Loss of muscle mass, strength and endurance
- Diminished bone mass and density

With age, women lose more bone than men and so are more susceptible to fractures from falling. Balance training and fall-prevention programmes, such as those in this book, are extremely beneficial to women and men, especially in this 'mature' stage of life. Some people are more likely to experience depression, loneliness and apprehension about change at this life stage. If you are not used to exercising, you may lack confidence about taking up a new activity.

The normal effects of ageing are compounded by a sedentary lifestyle.

How the GI Walking Diet Can Help

The mobility and strength programmes of the six-week plan will be invaluable. You don't have to spend hours doing them; they literally take minutes and you will reap significant benefits for your body. Many people may be widowed at this stage of life, and exercise offers a great opportunity to meet other people and socialize. Physical activity is known to have a positive effect on depression and mood, so get moving.

Aches and Pains

Some conditions, such as osteoporosis and arthritis, become more prevalent in later life, bringing us aches and pains. When these symptoms come to the surface, you may worry about how much exercise is actually achievable for you. However, the six-week programme addresses these concerns and allows you to tailor your programme to your abilities and needs. We look at some of the most common causes of aches and pains below.

Osteoporosis

Osteoporosis is a skeletal disease characterized by low bone mass, increased bone fragility and risk of fracture. Women are four times more likely to develop osteoporosis than men. Osteoporosis fractures occur most commonly in the hip, spine and wrist. Osteoporosis is often referred to as a silent disease because a fracture is frequently the first indication of bone loss.

How the GI Walking Diet Can Help

Diet and exercise can be both a treatment and prevention, as they help make your bones stronger. The impact to the bones due to walking makes it a great bone-saving exercise, so regular walking will help maintain strong bones. In addition to reducing bone loss, walking will improve muscle strength, balance, agility and fitness, making falls and fractures less likely. You should start slowly and gradually increase the amount you walk each week.

Walking has other life-enhancing psychological and cardiovascular benefits. Increased activity can aid nutrition, too, because it boosts appetite, which is often reduced in older people. It is also important to get enough calcium and vitamin D in your diet (see page 190). The biggest reason older people don't get enough of these is that they simply don't eat enough.

Arthritis

The term 'arthritis' refers to more than a hundred different diseases that cause pain, swelling and limited movement in joints and connective tissue throughout the body. Arthritis is usually a long-term condition, often lasting a lifetime. The three most prevalent types of arthritis are osteoarthritis, fibromyalgia and rheumatoid arthritis (see below).

Arthritis and other rheumatic conditions affect an estimated one in seven people. The number one cause of disability, arthritis can limit everyday activities such as dressing, climbing the stairs, getting in and out of bed and walking.

Overweight people are at greater risk of developing arthritis in their knees, hips and hands. The heaviest individuals have seven to ten times the risk of developing osteoarthritis of the knee. Weight control helps by decreasing the pressure on the knees and hips. Your walking technique can also reduce the force you apply through your hips and knees. We'll address this on page 65 with the really simple glass of water exercise.

How the GI Walking Diet Can Help

In the past, arthritis patients were advised to rest and avoid exercise. There is now strong evidence, however, for the benefits of exercise. While rest remains important, especially during flare-ups, inactivity can lead to weak muscles, stiff joints, a reduced range of motion in the joints and decreased energy and vitality. Most researchers agree that exercise can ease symptoms, but it is important to stress that it will neither cure nor prevent the condition.

Depending on your particular type of arthritis, you can choose which part of the six-week plan you would like to follow. The flexibility plan is a great place to start, while the strength plan may assist in building muscular strength, thus minimizing pressure on your joints. The walking plan can boost your spirits as well as aiding weight loss, again reducing pressure on weight-bearing joints such as knees, ankles and hips.

If your arthritis is severe, ease into the programme gently. You may not get the huge results you are initially looking for, but it's important to look beyond exercise purely for the benefit of your condition. People with arthritis are at higher risk of developing several other chronic diseases including heart disease, diabetes and osteoporosis. The huge health benefits of regular exercise will help prevent these diseases.

Osteoarthritis

The most common form of arthritis, osteoarthritis mostly affects people over the age of 45. Although this degenerative joint disease is common among older adults, it may appear decades earlier. Osteoarthritis begins when joint cartilage breaks down, sometimes eroding entirely, creating a bone-on-bone joint. The joint loses shape, bone ends thicken and spurs or bony growths develop. Although osteoarthritis can affect any joint, the most common are joints of the knee, hip, feet and fingers. Osteoarthritis is not fatal but it is incurable, with few effective treatments. Symptoms of pain and stiffness can persist for long periods, leading to difficulty in walking, climbing the stairs, rising from a chair, getting in and out of a car and lifting and carrying.

Fibromyalgia

Fibromyalgia sufferers experience general muscular pain, fatigue and poor sleep. Although it may feel like a joint disease, fibromyalgia is not a true form of arthritis and doesn't cause joint deformities. In fact, it is a form of soft tissue or muscular rheumatism.

Rheumatoid Arthritis

Rheumatoid arthritis, the third most common form of arthritis, is an auto-immune disease in which the body attacks itself. It is characterized by pain, warmth, redness and swelling. Many joints of the body have a tough capsule lined with a synovial membrane, which seals the joint and provides a lubricating fluid. In rheumatoid arthritis, inflammation begins in the synovial lining of the joint and can spread to the entire joint, leading to damage of the bone and cartilage. The space between joints diminishes and the joint loses shape and alignment.

Rheumatoid arthritis can strike at any age but usually appears between 20 and 50, developing slowly over several weeks or months. Although it is most often found in the small joints of the hands and the knee joint, it can affect most joints of the body. The effects of the disease vary widely: some people must remain in bed while others run marathons. It is also difficult to control and can cause severely deformed joints.

Other Forms of Arthritis

Other common types of arthritis include:

- **Gout**, a metabolic disorder that leads to high uric acid levels and crystal formation in joints, especially the big toe, and causes pain and swelling.
- **Spondylarthropathies**, inflammatory diseases of the spine that can result in fused vertebrae and a rigid spine.
- **Systemic lupus erythematosus**, an autoimmune disorder that can involve the skin, kidneys, blood vessels, joints, nervous system, heart and other internal organs. Although lupus can affect any part of the body, most people experience symptoms in only a few places. The most common symptoms are aching joints, skin rashes, anaemia, arthritis, prolonged fatigue and possible high fever. It is important to stress that diagnosis is made by a careful review of a person's entire medical history, coupled with a series of medical tests related to immune status. Currently, there is no single test that can determine whether a person has lupus or not.

Other Age-related Conditions

Hypertension (High Blood Pressure)

High blood pressure is strongly linked to cardiovascular disease and stroke. The risk of cardiovascular disease increases as blood pressure rises, even within the normal range of blood pressures. This suggests that a large number of people may be at risk.

How the GI Walking Diet Can Help

It's possible to reduce high blood pressure through physical activity, such as the six-week walking plan, and by adjusting your diet. The six-week menu plan is low in salt, making it ideal for people who need to reduce their blood pressure.

Diabetes

In diabetes, the body doesn't produce or cannot properly use insulin. Insulin is a hormone that converts sugar, starches and other foods into energy. Without insulin, glucose builds up in the bloodstream, and can lead to many health-threatening conditions. The health implications of diabetes are staggering:

- Diabetes is the leading cause of kidney disease.
- Diabetes is the main cause of new cases of blindness in people aged from 20 to 74 years.
- Sixty to seventy per cent of people with diabetes have mild-to-severe forms of diabetic nerve damage, which can lead to loss of lower limbs.
- People with diabetes are two to four times more likely to suffer from heart disease and strokes.

The exact cause of this long-term, incurable condition is a mystery. However, genetics and environmental factors – like obesity and lack of cardiovascular exercise – appear to play roles.

There are two types of diabetes:

- **Type 1 diabetes:** sufferers need daily insulin injections to stay alive because their body doesn't produce this hormone.
- **Type 2 diabetes:** the body makes insulin but is unable to produce enough or use it properly. Type 2 diabetes accounts for 90–95 per cent of all diabetes cases. It used to be referred to as 'late-onset diabetes', as it was more prevalent in later life. Now, however, with the growing number of overweight and obese people, type 2 diabetes is found even in young children. Doctors have warned that diabetes is nearing epidemic proportions.

Overweight people have a greater chance of developing type 2 diabetes, so keeping your weight under control is vital.

Metabolic Syndrome

In recent years, metabolic syndrome has become increasingly prevalent. A pre-diabetic condition, it is characterized by

- High triglyceride (blood fats) levels
- Elevated blood pressure
- High blood sugar levels
- Low levels of 'good' HDL cholesterol

and, guess what? That fat deposition in the middle again.

How the GI Walking Diet Can Help

Getting physically active and reducing your weight is the most important action you can take to prevent metabolic syndrome.

Every day is an opportunity to make a fresh start or to build on yesterday's success.

Ageing and Body Weight

Many different factors may have led to you putting on weight at this stage of your life. Some of these may have been physiological changes, while others may have been psychological issues. Understanding why this weight gain has occurred allows you to put things in context and to understand what action needs to be taken. Now is the time to get excited about what you can achieve for yourself, your body, your weight and your health.

Weight gain predominantly occurs because we are consuming more calories than we are burning off through physical activity. As we have seen, however, weight gain in later life can be the result of other factors, such as a decrease in our muscle mass and a consequent lowering of our resting metabolic rate. This leads to us requiring fewer calories to perform our everyday activities. In addition, hormonal changes make it easier for the body to lay down more fat, especially around the middle.

Why Men Lose Weight More Easily

I often hear people comment that it is much easier for a man to lose weight than it is for a woman. When partners embark on a 'diet' together, it is quite common for the man to lose weight more quickly, and possibly to lose a little more than his partner does. Research has shown that having personal support as you embark on a healthy lifestyle programme has a major impact on your long-term success. In fact, recovering male cardiac patients whose partners showed an active, positive, supportive role in their recovery had a 74 per cent greater success rate than patients whose partners showed neutral support.

From my research for this book, I know that many of you will want to complete the six-week plan with a partner or friend. I actively encourage people to do this. The walking plan, in particular, can be a great source of enjoyment. Walking with others can be great fun, and the support aspect will be vital when your motivation naturally wanes at points throughout the six weeks.

If, however, you are participating with members of the opposite sex, it is likely that your rate and amount of weight loss will be different. This doesn't mean that a woman's efforts are any less than a man's; the truth is there are strong physiological reasons why it is easier for men to lose weight. But before you give up before you have even started, let's make one thing clear – although your rate, and possibly the amount, of weight loss may be different, the health benefits to be gained are there for both men and women to enjoy.

> Although men tend to lose weight more easily, the health benefits of the GI Walking Diet are there for both men and women to enjoy.

How the Body Stores Fat

Most body fat is stored in fat cells called adipocytes. Around 50,000–60,000 calories of energy are stored as triglycerides in fat cells throughout the body, both under the skin and around the delicate organs. That's enough stored energy to walk briskly non-stop for 500–600 miles, or from London to Land's End. The body also stores fat between the muscle fibres, generally holding about 2,000–3,000 calories, enough to walk briskly non-stop for 20–30 miles. So before we even start to consume food for energy, our bodies are holding on to an awful lot of energy in the form of stored fat.

Where the fat is stored creates quite distinctive body shapes. Storage of body fat around the middle, resembling more of an apple or 'android shape', is characteristic among males and is associated with a higher risk of cardiovascular disease. Storage of body fat around the hips and thighs, creating a more rounded pear or 'gynoid' shape, is the most common body type among pre-menopausal women. The role of hormones in the way we store fat differs between men and women and affects how each lose weight.

Two hormones are particularly associated with fat distribution. Lipoprotein lipase (LPL) and hormone-sensitive lipase (HSL) directly affect whether we store fat or encourage it to be distributed in the blood and then burnt off. LPL tends to encourage fat storage, and HSL tends to encourage fat to be burnt off. The amount of LPL and HSL we have tends to vary between men and women, between individuals, in different areas of the body and at various stages of a woman's life. Men tend to have more LPL in the belly and less HSL in the lower hip area. This creates the more pronounced apple or android body shape seen in overweight men, with more body fat distributed around the belly. Women tend to have more LPL in the hips and backs of the arms and less HSL in the upper body. This classically creates more of the traditional pear or gynoid shape. When women lose weight, they generally still have more LPL in the hips so retain a pear shape, even though they may be a smaller pear shape.

It therefore seems obvious that getting more HSL can be only a good thing for aiding weight loss. HSL is stimulated by the hormone epinephrine, and what is really exciting is that exercise causes greater amounts of epinephrine to be released, and as you get fitter your body becomes more adept at using even small amounts of epinephrine to burn fat. So that's a great reason to get moving and keep moving.

A body that is significantly overweight or obese, however, will require higher amounts of epinephrine to stimulate fat-burning. For this reason it is vital that overweight people include gradual, progressive cardiovascular exercise into their weight-loss efforts. Walking is a fabulous way to do this.

The crucial difference between male and female fat loss is down to hormone receptors, which are located on the fat cell walls. There are two types of hormone receptor: alpha-receptors and beta-receptors. Alpha-receptors tend to inhibit fat breakdown while beta-receptors encourage it. Men and women don't have the same amount of these crucial hormone receptors. Men tend to have more of the fat-busting beta-receptors and fewer of the fat-storing alpha-receptors in their abdomen, while women tend to have fewer beta-receptors and more alpha-receptors. The more beta-receptors there are in the abdomen, the easier it is to lose middle-age spread. So when a man loses weight, it will be easier for him to drop inches off the midriff area than it would be for a woman. Finally, the last infuriating piece of evidence that it's easier for men to lose weight is that, even at rest, a man will be burning more calories than a woman. This is because their fat cells are smaller than women's!

The Oestrogen Effect

Another factor in the weight-loss battle of the sexes relates to the female sex hormone oestrogen. Oestrogen has an impact on fat storage in a number of ways:

- It encourages epinephrine production, which helps the breakdown of fat
- It prevents the fat-storing LPL from working as effectively
- It encourages the production of growth hormone, which increases the release of fatty acids from the fat cells
- It is also thought to inhibit the production of insulin, encouraging the body to use fat rather than glucose as a source of energy

During menopause, however, the amount of oestrogen decreases, so its ability to help break down fat is diminished. This causes weight gain in the midriff to become more prevalent in women than in men.

It's not all doom and gloom, however, as oestrogen also increases the production of nitric oxide, which encourages the blood vessels to relax. High nitric oxide concentrations are associated with migraine, and it is often reported that migraine sufferers experience less frequent and severe migraines after menopause.

Weight Gain and Stress

Stress is another factor that can lead to weight gain and middle-age spread. Scientists are just beginning to discover that long-term emotional stress can contribute to age-related weight gain, especially in older women.

For more on stress and other emotional challenges, see Chapter 2.

How the GI Walking Diet Can Help

You will lose weight on the GI Walking Diet. The combination of the physical activity and eating plans allows you to follow a flexible or more structured approach to your goal. All you have to do is choose which approach suits you, and you are on your way to losing 5–10 per cent of your excess body weight. Losing weight can be an intimidating process – sometimes the amount of weight we feel we have to lose can be off-putting – but the positive news is that even a small amount of weight loss can improve your health. In fact, research shows that a drop of just 6 per cent will significantly improve your health.

If you are carrying excess weight, an initial goal of losing 5–10 per cent of your starting weight is both realistic and valuable. Plus, by following the six-week plan, you will be more likely to keep the weight off, maintaining your health improvements.

> If I said to you – in six weeks from today you could be 6 per cent lighter, far healthier, fitter and energetic, wouldn't you want to take action?

2 Emotional Challenges

Life's too short to sweat the small stuff.

Can your emotions affect your health? Evidence now suggests the answer is 'yes'. One study of pre-menopausal, peri-menopausal and post-menopausal women found that emotions like anger, depression and anxiety increase the risk of developing metabolic syndrome (see page 28). Other studies have confirmed that long-term stress causes the shape-shifting phenomenon of middle-age spread due to too much sugar being converted to fat, which gets deposited in the midriff area. Researchers have also established a link between stress and poor health. And, of course, when we are stressed, sad, angry, afraid, hurt, worried, lonely, frustrated or depressed we reach for food as a source of emotional comfort.

Emotional Stress

Most experts define emotional stress as a person's reaction to any situation that places special physical or psychological demands on them so as to unbalance their equilibrium and take them outside their comfort zone. These situations can give rise to feelings of fear, anger or anxiety as the body responds to the perceived threat to its wellbeing. Emotional stress varies from person to person so is difficult to measure. It is highly subjective and influenced by personality and experience; everyone has a different sensitivity to stressful events – what may be stressful to one person can be perceived as quite manageable to another.

The concept of emotional stress pioneered by Dr Hans Seyle proposes that during stressful situations, the sympathetic nervous system sets in motion a series of physiological responses. Various hormones produced by the adrenal cortex, including cortisol and epinephrine, prepare the body for an instant state of readiness, the classic 'fight or flight' response. It is also theorized that once the 'stress-invoking threat' has passed, the body returns to a state of normality and balance. However, recent research shows that long-term elevated cortisol levels can lead to weight gain, especially in the belly.

Although both men and women may be uncomfortable with some of the changes to their faces and bodies as they get older, women often feel more vulnerable as society places such a high value on their physical appearance. For women over 40, excess weight can become more difficult to shift, and this is often compounded by emotional challenges. At this stage of life, emotional issues that have been suppressed for years can resurface. Additionally, divorce, financial burdens, concerns about retirement, career moves and residential changes often occur alongside unpleasant menopausal symptoms. With the children now grown up and out of the family home, many people begin to question their own identity, which was typically being the family caregiver. This loss of identity can be unsettling for many, and may coincide with a new role of becoming the 'parent' to their own ill or ageing parents.

Emotional challenges can be difficult at any age. In later life, emotional stress can be harder to deal with if we are no longer physically fit and healthy. Coping with an age-related medical condition – such as arthritis, diabetes, high blood pressure, heart disease or osteoporosis – can be a considerable burden. Physical problems combined with emotional challenges – such as periods of mourning, feelings of increased isolation in retirement and a changing social role – can all contribute to a sense of loss of control and helplessness. This makes people vulnerable to depression.

Emotional Eating

We all know food can make us feel good, providing a great source of psychological fulfilment. From infancy, we are taught that love and food are intertwined. A baby cries – we feed it to calm it down; a child does well and is rewarded with a food treat; and of course seduction and food have been entwined since Creation – just think of Adam and Eve! In later life we have a whole catalogue of food memories associated with holidays, celebrations and happy times, so it's really no wonder that we equate food with positive feelings. When emotionally stressed, some people strive to recapture those happy feelings by comforting themselves with food. It has recently been shown that we are more likely to engage in emotional eating if our basic human needs – such as security, love and belonging – are unfulfilled. Prolonged periods of depression and anxiety also tend to cause emotional eating, leading to cravings for sweet and fatty foods.

> Many parents and grandparents mistakenly use food as a reward for positive behaviour: 'If you are a good girl or boy today you will get a treat.' This strategy may create a lasting unconscious desire to reward oneself with sweet, high-calorie foods when under emotional stress. This may develop into unhealthy eating habits, so that being overweight becomes a self-fulfilling prophecy. Aim to reward younger members of the family with non-food treats, such as a trip to a park, a treasure hunt or a physical activity. This will have a much more positive impact on their health.

Why People Eat Emotionally

In my experience with both female and male clients, people often find themselves trapped in a cycle of stress-eat-stress, feeling helpless to change. Significant weight gain can occur as a result. There may be unconscious reasons for this behaviour. You may want to prevent other people getting too close, and feel that a layer of fat on the body may protect you. Or it can represent an attitude of needing to let go and be out of control when all other aspects of your life have to be neat and in order.

Case Study

A male client, a city high-flyer, had a major problem with emotional eating late in the evening. After working with him for a month it became clear that the nature of his professional position meant he had to be in control and on top of his game 110 per cent of the time. There was no room for a slip-up. This was big business with big rewards. The client was exceedingly good at his job, but it came at a price to his health – 5 stone of excess weight gain. Although he ate healthily, and in moderation at work, it was all part of his professional approach. When he came home it was almost as if some element of being out of control was needed as light relief from the constant responsibility and challenges. Ice cream was the answer, and his excessive eating of it represented a rebellious act against all the constraints in his day-to-day life. After discussing this, we established a physical activity plan that introduced an element of stress management, as well as letting him create a little slack in other areas of his life, so that the ice cream eating was not his only outlet to let off steam and take his foot off the throttle.

Emotional stress is real, and it doesn't go away quickly or simply. However, recognizing it is the first step to taking action. If you feel you are susceptible to emotional stress, try completing the following questionnaire. Often, it can be easier to express sensitive issues on paper rather than in a face-to-face discussion. You may find that the very act of completing the questionnaire provokes thought and introspection, creating an awareness of the role stress is playing in your life.

Emotional Stress Questionnaire

Using the scale below, rate the following items/events according to how frequently they cause you emotional stress in the form of sadness, anxiety, fear, anger, depression, worry or guilt:

1 – Never

2 – Occasionally (a few times a month or less)

3 – Sometimes (one to three times a week)

4 – Often (three or more times a week)

5 – Always (daily or more)

- Job-related issues (unhappy with/change in/losing job) 1 2 3 4 5
- Children (leaving/returning home, marital difficulties) 1 2 3 4 5
- Relationship issues with loved ones 1 2 3 4 5
- Separation or divorce 1 2 3 4 5
- A new relationship 1 2 3 4 5
- Loneliness 1 2 3 4 5
- Concerns about personal health 1 2 3 4 5
- Illness or death of a parent, close relative or friend 1 2 3 4 5
- Thoughts about retirement 1 2 3 4 5
- Worrying about finances 1 2 3 4 5

- ◆ Food and eating 1 2 3 4 5
- ◆ Your physical appearance/body weight 1 2 3 4 5
- ◆ Your physical activity levels 1 2 3 4 5
- ◆ Moving home 1 2 3 4 5
- ◆ Feelings of general unhappiness 1 2 3 4 5
- ◆ Other _____ 1 2 3 4 5

Answer the following questions:

- ◆ Have you experienced any recent or sudden weight gain?   YES/NO
- ◆ Do you have frequent, general feelings of sadness, anxiety, loneliness, despair, resentment, anger, guilt, shame, boredom or fear?   YES/NO
- ◆ Have these feelings interfered with your normal daily functioning, including lifestyle habits such as healthy eating, regular exercise, not smoking, drinking alcohol only in moderation?   YES/NO
- ◆ Do you reach for food when feeling emotionally stressed?   YES/NO
- ◆ If yes, what sort of food do you usually reach for?

  _____

- ◆ Do you feel better after eating these foods?   YES/NO
- ◆ Are you a (circle one) binge-eater/chronic dieter/emotional eater/purger?
- ◆ Do you have difficulty sleeping?   YES/NO
- ◆ Are you (circle one) pre-/peri-/post-menopausal?
- ◆ Do you experience any menopausal symptoms?   YES/NO
- ◆ If so, are they severe enough to interfere with daily living?   YES/NO
- ◆ Are you (circle one): happy | somewhat satisfied | dissatisfied – with your current body weight?
- ◆ Do you regularly participate in any stress-relieving activities, such as listening to relaxation tapes, meditating or attending mind-body classes (such as yoga or t'ai chi), or do you participate in individual or group counselling sessions with a social worker or other mental health professional?   YES/NO
- ◆ Are you taking any anti-anxiety/anti-depression medication?   YES/NO

How You Answered

The purpose of the first part of this questionnaire is to raise your awareness of certain issues or factors that can cause you stress. The second part is designed to highlight how you respond to specific events or situations.

Raising your level of regular physical activity – especially when it involves getting outside, as in the walking plan – has been shown to be a highly effective way to combat stress and limit depression. If your answers to the questionnaire highlighted several areas that could be improved, I'd encourage you to revisit the questionnaire after you have completed the six-week plan.

Breaking the cycle of emotional stress can be hard, but the number one message to remember is that exercise – specifically cardiovascular activity – is a powerful tamer of emotional stress. Your six-week walking plan will help you alleviate anxiety and depression and boost self-esteem. You will lose excess body fat and feel more confident. So not only are you going to look better, you will feel better too.

As well as exercising, allocating a little time for yourself to engage in some form of self-nurture that doesn't involve food can have a positive impact on how you feel about yourself. You could, for example, take a class, read or relax in the bath ...

3 Making it Happen – Changing Habits and Attitudes

Would you rather exercise for an hour a day – or be dead for 24 hours a day? Think about it…

If you are serious about losing weight and improving your health, you have to make some changes. Don't panic – these don't have to be drastic. However, these changes will essentially involve your existing habits and attitudes. At this stage in your life, your habits and attitudes will be well developed; you have had many years to put them into practice. Your habits may be so well grooved that they are a permanent feature of your life. They feel natural and you don't give them much thought. For example, that mid-afternoon cup of tea and slice of cake or biscuit, your daily stroll with the dog, pint down the pub or G and T in the evening.

Get Active!

Evidence has shown that we tend to overestimate how physically active we are. As I explained in the Introduction, many of us believe we are physically active when in fact we are geographically or mentally active (see page vi). You may need to rethink and readjust your habits. For instance, you may believe that your daily saunter with the dog is enough for your fitness. It's not that everyday activities are ineffective: the Chief Medical Officer's report, 'Health of the Nation', clearly stated that activities such as walking and gardening are sufficient to incur health benefits. The problem, however, is that they are often not vigorous enough to produce real health benefits, let alone weight loss.

In my research for this book, time and time again respondents believed they were 'doing enough' and that they were 'physically active'. On closer examination, however, the intensity and progression needed to provide health improvements and weight loss were missing. Seventy per cent of the respondents said the changes they primarily sought were weight loss and health improvements. Despite putting in time and effort to improve their health, they didn't achieve the results they sought. This lack of results creates a sense of frustration and an element of 'what's the use?'

So, on your six-week plan, you may need to develop some new habits and attitudes. The great news is that some of the core habits you need may already be in place, but just need a little tweaking.

> Stop kidding yourself you are doing enough
> and start making your actions count.

Your attitude can directly affect your health and ageing process, either positively or negatively. By adjusting your habits and educating your attitudes, the actions you take become not only achievable but also sustainable, making the whole ageing process a far more positive experience. Together, all your habits and attitudes can lead you to an achievable major change to your health, your weight and how you feel about yourself.

Small Steps for Big Change

To help you understand how you can make your existing habits and attitudes work for you, we need to introduce the concept of 'small steps for big change', which is central to the success of the six-week plan. This means that all the small actions you take, when put together and done progressively, can lead to a big change in your health and weight.

So often, I see people who are committed to improving their health but their actions fail. This is because their expectations are too great, and the changes they are trying to put in place are too drastic, unrealistic and unachievable for them. The six-week plan is about achievability, and the small steps for big change concept will be crucial to your success.

> The six-week plan is about *achievability* and *taking small steps to make a big change*.

What Is a Habit?

A habit is a series of behaviours we have got used to doing in response to a specific cue. When trying to adopt a new, healthy regime, we can often come unstuck as we try to ditch too many habits too quickly, and implement new actions which bear no resemblance to our existing life. Such a large change can be daunting, difficult to maintain and often leads to us dropping all the good

actions we need to take. Implementing new habits does involve some planning and thought, but the new habits I am going to ask you to develop need
not be a world away from some of the ones you already have.

To help us make habit-changing an achievable process, we need to understand a little about how we form habits.

Habit-forming in the Brain

Understanding how the brain works provides us with an insight into our
behaviour and how habits are formed. Here is a very simple overview of how
habits are formed in the brain.

The brain is responsible for receiving, processing and sending out messages
based on vast amounts of information. Message carriers called neurons need
to travel to specific destinations in the brain so that the information can be
acted upon. The message carriers reach their destinations by travelling along
neural pathways; you can think of these as a mini transport system. There are
millions and millions of neurons in the brain, all carrying messages and travelling along neural pathways. Different parts of the brain deal with different types
of information. If the message goes to the wrong part of the brain or doesn't
reach its correct destination, the information gets lost, never to be acted upon.

At their destination, the neurons deliver their message, the information gets
processed and an action may or may not occur. The brain gets very good at
doing the simplest thing – taking a message and sending it along the most
accessible neural pathway, delivering its message and creating an action. Some
of these actions get so familiar that they become an automatic response, which
requires no conscious thinking. When this happens you have given birth to
a habit.

Other bits of information never reach their specific destination, so the part of the brain responsible for carrying out a particular action becomes dormant. Your brain may receive the same information again and again, but each time the message carrier gets lost in the smaller back roads of the brain, never to reach its destination.

Now you can start to see why taking small steps can be so effective. If your brain is already doing a similar action, the transport system taking the information will be established. Making a tweak to that action is easier for your brain to process and develop than trying to do a totally new action that requires the neuron message carriers to travel along unfamiliar neural pathways to a destination that may be dormant.

In this way, grooving the new habits necessary to help you lose weight and improve your health need not be that difficult. The trick is to piggy-back your new habit on to something you are already doing. For example, one of the most popular forms of physical activity is walking. We know from research studies that walking can improve your health and help you lose weight and keep it off, but the way you are walking at the moment may not be sufficient for you to reap these benefits. So the one simple habit you need to evolve may not be miles away from what you are already doing. All you need to do is address your walking technique and pace. You'll find really simple and effective ways to do this on page 64.

Not all of your existing habits will be beneficial to your health, and it is likely that some of your habits may need to be ditched. However, eating the odd bar of chocolate or indulging in a cream tea once a week is not a bad habit – it's when these 'weekly' habits are more of a daily habit that action needs to be taken.

Since we all have individual habits that directly affect our health and wellbeing, we need to apply a good dose of truthfulness. In my experience with clients, it can be very helpful to put these actions into context, and introduce an element of reality into how many times you actually complete the behaviour.

Habit Reality Check

Here's what you do:
- Carry out an activity audit. Make a list of 10 'physical activity behaviours' you do regularly, such as a keep fit class, walking the dog or walking to the shops.
- For each of these behaviours, complete the following Habit Reality Check questionnaire. Rate your responses on a scale of 0–7, 0 being 'agree strongly' and 7 being 'disagree strongly'.

(Behaviour X) is something:
- I do frequently   1 2 3 4 5 6 7
- I do automatically   1 2 3 4 5 6 7
- I do without having to consciously remember   1 2 3 4 5 6 7
- that makes me feel weird if I don't do it   1 2 3 4 5 6 7
- I do without thinking   1 2 3 4 5 6 7
- would require effort not to do   1 2 3 4 5 6 7
- that belongs to my (daily, weekly, monthly) routine   1 2 3 4 5 6 7
- I start doing before I realize I'm doing it   1 2 3 4 5 6 7
- I would find hard not to do   1 2 3 4 5 6 7
- I have no need to think about doing   1 2 3 4 5 6 7
- that's typically 'me'   1 2 3 4 5 6 7
- I have been doing for a long time   1 2 3 4 5 6 7

Please note: some of the above statements may need to be adapted according to the nature of the behaviour. However, the main purpose of this exercise is to draw your attention to some of your actions, which may be overlooked.

Case Study

Fifteen years ago I was running weight-management programmes in the US. One particular female client in her early 50s continually struggled with her weight. Each week, this client would swear to me that she'd had no sweets or treats at all and was following a healthy and moderate-calorie eating plan. Interestingly, however, on three separate occasions I saw her driving away from the building with one hand on the steering wheel and the other in a bumper packet of sweets. It's not for me to say that this client was telling untruths, but sometimes you do need to give yourself a good reality check and get a grip of what's happening. When I took this client through the Habit Reality Check, the fifth point was particularly pertinent.

Have I Left it Too Late?

So you've picked up this book and now you're thinking: this is all really depressing; what's the point? I might as well not bother; I've left it far too late. Well, before you crawl into Victor Meldrew mode, let's get one thing straight:

NO – it really is never too late to start!!

So don't even go there as an excuse – your efforts can make a real and positive impact on the quality of your life. In fact, most studies indicate that untrained people, even in the eighth decade of life, have not lost the ability to adapt to aerobic exercise training such as the walking plan. It's never too late to improve, and now the time has come for you to prove it to yourself. The same basic exercise programmes used for young adults can be applied in later life, but there will be a slightly different emphasis upon what you do and how you progress, depending on your age and ability.

The benefits are there for you to enjoy. The exciting thing is that you have more to gain now than at any other stage of life. Your body will reward you more for your efforts and the time you invest in your body. So let's start working towards these achievable goals for losing weight, improving your health and, most important of all, feeling better about yourself.

II

Opening the Window of Opportunity

Ability is what you are capable of doing.
Motivation determines what you do

4 How the GI Walking Diet Works

Arriving at one goal is the starting point for another.

The GI Walking Diet has two main components: the exercise plan and the eating plan. Each has been devised specifically to help you improve your health, lose weight, get rid of middle-age spread and boost your energy using the concept of 'small steps for big change'. In this chapter I will provide an overview of the plan. It's important that you understand how the plan works so you can appreciate that your actions will reap rewards. You need to feel confident that you are following a programme based on scientific evidence that is results-orientated and achievable for you. In Chapters 6 and 7 you will find the week-by-week exercise and menu plans.

The Exercise Plan

Your exercise plan has three parts. Each targets an essential aspect of health:

1. The walking plan improves your cardiovascular stamina and endurance
2. The strength plan maintains your bone density and works in conjunction with your
3. Flexibility programme, to improve your agility, mobility and balance

Combined, these three programmes over the six weeks will:
- Improve your posture
- Increase your energy
- Enhance your wellbeing
- Achieve sustainable weight loss and significantly change your body shape

Each plan is clearly laid out, detailing exactly what you need to do each week. The exercises in each plan will progress a little from week to week. This is important so your body gets fitter and you reap optimum results from your efforts. You get to choose when you complete each plan and on which days. Remember, the overall aim of the six-week plan is to improve your lifestyle as a whole through increases in physical activity that can be incorporated on a regular basis, not just for the duration of the six weeks. Your results will be achievable but they will also be sustainable.

Your walking plan needs to be completed on five days out of seven. However, as you will see, the goal is to improve your overall walking distance throughout the day – you won't have to set aside large parts of the day to achieve your goals. Your strength and flexibility plans need to be completed on three days each week. Again, you can choose when you do this, but don't leave it to chance: get organized and plan, otherwise you may find yourself at the end

of the week without achieving your goals. This not only takes some of the
pleasure away but can also prevent you from getting the maximum benefits.
In my experience, it is helpful to plan out when each exercise session will take
place, so on pages 161–6 I have provided you with a week-by-week plan.
You'll also find lots of suggestions and guidance, based on both practical experience and scientific research, to help you get the most from your efforts.

Remember, the greatest change comes about by doing small things on a regular and consistent basis – your small steps for big change. That is why I have
designed each plan to be as flexible and time-efficient as possible. You can read
more about each plan – what it involves, why and how you do it and the benefits to your body – in Chapter 6.

Walk Your Way to Weight Loss and Health

Walking is central to your six-week plan.

> If a daily fitness walk could be packaged in a pill, it would be one of the most
> popular prescriptions in the world.

It has so many health benefits it's difficult to know where to begin. In fact,
you may be quite sceptical, having heard so many claims about various forms
of exercise that have been the fashion over the years. But there is no disputing
the facts: walking can reduce the risk of many diseases – from heart attacks
and strokes to hip fractures and glaucoma – and just about anyone can benefit. These may sound like claims on a dubious bottle of pills but there is no
disputing the science, as the benefits are backed by major research. Walking
requires no prescription, the risk of side-effects is very low, and the benefits
are numerous. Here are just a few:

- **Managing your weight.** Combined with healthy eating, physical activity is key to any plan for long-lasting weight control. Keeping your weight within healthy limits can lower your risk of type 2 diabetes, heart disease, stroke, cancer, sleep apnoea and osteoarthritis.

- **Controlling your blood pressure.** Physical activity strengthens the heart so it can pump more blood with less effort and with less pressure on the arteries. Staying fit is just as effective as some medications in keeping down blood pressure levels.

- **Decreasing your risk of a heart attack.** Exercise such as brisk walking for three hours a week – or just half an hour a day – is associated with a 30–40 per cent reduction in the risk of heart disease in women. (Based on the Nurses' Health Study, a 20-year study of 72,000 female nurses.)

- **Boosting the level of high-density lipoproteins (HDL), known as 'good' cholesterol.** Physical activity helps reduce the 'bad' low-density lipoprotein (LDL) cholesterol in the blood, which can cause a build-up of plaque along the artery walls – a major cause of heart attacks.

- **Lowering your risk of stroke.** Regular, moderate exercise equivalent to brisk walking for an hour a day, five days a week, can cut the risk of stroke in half, according to a Harvard study of more than 11,000 men.

- **Reducing your risk of breast cancer and type 2 diabetes.** The Nurses' Health Study also linked regular activity to reductions in the risk of both these diseases. In another study, people at high risk of diabetes cut their risk in half by combining consistent exercise like walking with a lower fat intake and a 5–7 per cent weight loss.

- **Avoiding gallstone surgery.** Regular walking or other physical activity lowers the risk of needing gallstone surgery by 20–31 per cent. (Based on a Harvard Medical School study of more than 60,000 women aged 40–65.)

- **Protecting against hip fracture.** Consistent physical activity diminishes the risk of hip fracture, concludes a study of more than 30,000 men and women aged 20–93.
- **Helps with sleep problems.** (See below.)

The advantages go on and on. Many other studies indicate a daily brisk walk also can help:

- Prevent depression, colon cancer, constipation, osteoporosis and impotence
- Lengthen lifespan
- Lower stress levels
- Relieve arthritis and back pain
- Strengthen muscles, bones and joints
- Elevate overall mood and sense of wellbeing

Walk to Sleep Like a Log

In my research for this book, over 70 per cent of respondents cited lack of sleep as a problem. Whether it's fitful sleeping or waking in the night, lack of sleep can be both upsetting and depressing, and can directly affect your body shape. But you can have a more relaxing night by being more physically active throughout the day.

A full night of good sleep is important to your overall wellbeing, and being active can improve your sleep cycle. When you sleep well, you wake feeling more rested and alert. Daily walks can relieve insomnia and other sleep disorders by:

- Loosening tight muscles
- Reducing stress

- Promoting longer, deeper sleep periods known as slow wave – the phase of sleep that helps restore the body
- Lessening symptoms of depression and anxiety

It's no surprise that the quality and length of your sleep affects how you feel. It has been scientifically proven that good, sound sleep is necessary for health:

- University of Chicago researchers found that lack of sleep reduces the amount of human growth hormone. This hormone is responsible for the body's fat-to-muscle ratio. Restful sleep creates a balance of the hormone and leads to better health.
- When you haven't slept well, your body craves energy, which causes a release of glucose into the bloodstream. This slows your metabolism and can cause weight gain. Good sleep, on the other hand, helps you maintain a healthy metabolism.

Without enough sleep, you feel sluggish and tired and you don't want to exercise. The result is a negative cycle that leads to many problems. Instead, walking can create a positive cycle for your body with the right balance of sleep and exercise. It works both ways: activity helps satisfy your body's need for sleep, and a better sleep pattern motivates you to keep moving.

Tips to Help You Walk to Sleep

◆ Ease yourself into your six-week walking plan. Move at a pace that's right for you. Walk as far and for as long as is comfortable, working up to longer, brisker walks. Introducing activity steadily gives your body time to get used to it. This reduces the chances of sore muscles – a common excuse for giving up too quickly.

◆ Try taking a short stroll before and after dinner. These steps can go towards your accumulated daily target, and will help soothe your nerves while burning calories. The use of energy combined with the stress release relaxes your body and mind, helping you sleep better and longer.

◆ Once you're used to walking, keep this in mind: the ideal walk is brisk enough to make you break into a sweat, but not so fast that you run out of breath. Make the last bit of your walk slower. This brings your heartbeat down to its resting rate, which prepares your body for a decent night's sleep.

◆ On restless nights, get up and pace around the house instead of turning on the television. Take in deep breaths as you move. Shake out your arms and legs, and stretch out your neck. When you climb back into bed, you'll feel more prepared to fall asleep. If your mind is racing, try my 'still eyes' exercise. When the mind races, your eyes flicker, reflecting the activity of your brain. If you can still your eyes, you will find you will be able to still the mind. Lie face-up, eyes shut. Keeping your eyes shut, cast them down towards your navel, focusing your attention on that one spot. Take five deep breaths as you keep your eyes drawn towards the navel. Notice that as your mind starts to wander, so does your eye line. Try to keep the eyes directed towards the navel, and focus on letting them soften and fall away from your eyelids. All the time, be aware of your breath. If sleep trouble persists, have a chat with your GP about it. Sleep tight!

Creating a walking plan that is achievable for you is essential to your success. From my research for this book, I know many people are already walking, but the amount and intensity varies considerably. This has a direct bearing on their results. Other people are non-walkers, perhaps put off by hip replacement operations, excess weight or just not knowing where to start.

> The six-week walking plan has two levels: the **entry level** and the **advanced level.** Following either level will increase your fitness, boost your energy and improve your health, but you get to choose the plan that suits your personal needs and rate of progression.
>
> - Non-walkers or people new to walking should follow the entry level plan.
> - Those who are more used to physical exercise are advised to follow the advanced plan.
>
> Both will guide you through an achievable and results-orientated programme. You'll be accumulating your steps throughout the day as well as introducing intensity walking, which is crucial to the success of your weight loss efforts.

The '10,000 Steps a Day' Message

The Japanese slogan '10,000 steps a day' has gained popularity in both the UK and the US. Many experts believe that taking 10,000 steps a day, measured with a good pedometer, is all that's necessary to achieve health, weight loss and fitness improvements. However, although taking 10,000 steps a day will improve your health, it may not have a significant impact on your weight loss or fitness, unless it is performed in the correct way. This causes me considerable concern as I often receive letters from people feeling despondent that their walking efforts do not reap results. They end up feeling frustrated and on the verge of giving up, which is the last thing they should do!

How Many Steps Do You Need to Take?

- **For health:** accumulate your 10,000 steps daily. Depending on how much walking you already do, this will probably involve going for a structured walk. Anything less than 5,000 steps a day is classified as physically inactive.
- **For fitness:** you need to push yourself a little harder to see improvements in the stamina of your heart and lungs. Aim to walk in bouts of at least 10 minutes and push yourself so you get slightly out of breath each time. Play with your break point (see page 66) or find some hills to stride up.
- **For weight loss:** this partly depends on how much physical activity you are doing already, but studies carried out on the Amish community in the US suggest that without adjusting diet, daily step targets may need to be in the region of 16,000. For best results, combine timed brisk-paced walks with daily accumulated targets.

One of the aims of the GI Walking Diet is to help you lose weight, so you will be combining daily step targets measured on a pedometer with some intensity walking. In conjunction with your eating plan, this will help you achieve and sustain a 6 per cent loss of excess weight.

Your Physical Activity Level

American pedometer experts have proposed a 'steps per day index' for determining your physical activity level based on accumulated steps with your pedometer. Based on this index, 10,000 steps appear to be an appropriate target for everyone to work towards for health improvements. However, it is difficult for anyone to accumulate 10,000 steps without some sort of continuous walking activity. Government guidelines for physical activity aimed at reducing chronic disease advise all adults to accumulate at least 30 minutes of moderate physical activity, such as brisk walking, on most – if not all – days of the week. Ideally, adults should accumulate the 30 minutes in continuous bouts lasting for at least 10 minutes. Research has demonstrated that adults who clock up 10,000 steps a day are more likely to meet the 30-minute recommendation.

Steps per Day Physical Activity Index for Adults

Steps/day	Physical Activity (Pedometer-determined) Level
Less than 5,000	Sedentary
5,000-7,499	Low active
7,500-9,999	Somewhat Active
10,000-12,499	Active
More than 12,500	Highly Active

What You Need

Walking is so simple, easy and accessible that you don't need to spend a fortune. In fact, it's just about the cheapest form of physical activity you can do. However, there are a few things you can do before you start to make your walking plan a lot more achievable:

- Invest in a good pedometer
- Learn your walking technique
- Find the right pace for you
- Establish your baseline number of steps
- Get a comfortable pair of shoes

Invest in a Good Pedometer

Not all pedometers are created equal. Studies have shown accuracy varies by as much as 37 per cent. This is a huge element of error and potential cause of mis-information about how physically active you truly are. Ideally, the level of error should be within 0–3 per cent, the industry standard in Japan. This means if you walk 100 steps, the pedometer should read 97–103. You can easily test the accuracy of a pedometer: simply wear it on your belt, according to the manu-facturer's instructions, and walk 100 steps, counting as you go. If the pedometer reads less than 97 or more than 103, repeat the test. If it fails again, ditch it and get a better one. A few pedometers are accurate on a purposeful walk but don't count well during normal daily movement like walking from your front door to the car or around your office. Other accurate pedometers last only a month or two before the little pieces inside wear out and the accuracy is lost.

Having used such a variety of pedometers over the years, I know how impor-tant it is to have a good model, and I have seen some very poor ones! Since I feel so strongly about the health value of a good pedometer, I recommend only one pedometer, which is one I have developed myself. It has an error level of 1 per cent, compared to the industry's accepted standard of a 3 per cent error. This means that if you walk 100 steps, counting as you go, my pedometer should read 99–101. There are no fiddly functions as these tend to reduce the accuracy. Most important of all, it is easy to use. There are two models available: one measures just your steps and the other measures your steps and distance. Which you choose is entirely up to you, but you also have a choice of colour as there are seven to choose from! You can buy one of my pedometers through my website: www.joannahall.com.

Getting the Most from Your Pedometer

- Many pedometers appear to be most accurate at a walking speed of 80 metres per minute or about 3 miles per hour (mph) (actually 2.98mph).
- Normal walking speed for most people is 2–4.5 mph.
- The slower the walking speed, the more inaccurate the step count. This may be because the vertical accelerations of the waist (the pendulum movements) are less pronounced at slower speeds. Also, stride length may be too short for the pedometer to register.
- Whether a pedometer is worn on the left or right side doesn't appear to affect accuracy.
- Excess fat at the waist may create inaccuracy.
- Distance and calorie expenditure are estimated from the step data, using manufacturers' formulas. Some pedometers are more accurate than others, and I wouldn't personally recommend the accuracy of pedometers with calorie functions.
- Generally, distance is less accurate than step count.

As well as being accurate and easy to use, a pedometer should be well-made and reliable. The main issue here is whether the pedometer will break easily or run out of battery life quickly. Lots of cheaper models have a problem with battery life – they are made in China and use cheap components, including batteries. The best pedometers use watch batteries, available from any watch shop, which last around three years with normal use. Cheaper pedometers can also break easily, especially around the clip. To my mind a pedometer needs a cover – without a cover your pedometer will easily get reset, just by bending over or knocking it with your arm, thus losing count of how many steps you have taken that day. Ideally, the cover should not be too stiff and can act as a useful disguise if you are conscious about wearing a pedometer – many people will then think it is a pager.

The accuracy of your pedometer depends on two elements: where you position it and your stride length.

Positioning Your Pedometer

- The device must sit on the waistband or belt so it is horizontal and straight. If the pedometer tilts, it becomes inaccurate.
- It should align with the middle of the thigh, or about 4 to 5 inches from the belly button (depending on body type).
- A pedometer won't work in a pocket because it can't stay vertical. However, one manufacturer says that hanging it from a lanyard (a cord worn around the neck) will work.

Stride Length Input

Not all pedometers require you to enter stride length, but if they do, here are some tips:

- Walk with a normal gait when measuring your step length.

- Note that step length decreases when you walk uphill and increases when you walk downhill. If you are doing a lot of hill-walking and want to measure your steps accurately, you will need to adjust the stride length programmed into the pedometer. However, my view is that you don't need to worry about this when you are getting started on your walking plan.

- Try using water to measure your footprints. Outside on concrete, pour water into a puddle and splash around to get the bottoms of your shoes wet. Then measure your wet footprints from left heel strike to right heel strike. If you measure in inches, divide by 12 to get the number of feet.

- Walk a measured track where you know the distance, and count your steps. Then divide the distance by the number of steps to get your stride length.

- Measure a 3–6 metre (10–20 foot) distance and walk it several times, counting steps, to get the average number of steps for the distance. Divide distance by steps to calculate stride length.

Pedometer Trivia

Pedometers aren't the new device you may think they are. In the 15th century, Leonardo da Vinci left drawings that indicate he designed a device with a pendulum arm to measure steps. Thomas Jefferson, an early US president, used a pedometer he purchased in France.

Learn Your Walking Technique

When you're walking for weight loss, your technique is especially important. Mastering a good walking technique takes some time but, with practice, it will become second nature and help you increase and maintain your pace comfortably.

Form and Posture

Good form will help you walk faster and longer, increasing your fitness level more quickly. You'll tire less easily, use more of your core abdominal and back muscles, and improve the overall efficiency of your workout.

- **Strike with the heel first.** Your heel should hit the ground first. Roll your foot through to the toe, with no unnatural pushing from one foot to the other. Take shorter, rather than longer, steps; more frequent short steps will give you a better workout and be easier on your joints.

- **Swing your arms.** Bend your arms at the elbow at a 90-degree angle and swing them towards the centre of your body. Be careful not to cross the centre line of your body or bend your arms more than 90 degrees. Swinging your arms properly will give you a better aerobic workout, burn more calories, and engage more muscles throughout your torso. Also, you will be able to move faster than if your arms are dangling at your sides. Just keep your hands in a lightly curled fist but avoid clenching as this raises blood pressure.

- **Stretch your spine.** To maintain good posture, stretch your spine tall, reaching up to the sky with the top of your head. Your head should be resting comfortably in line with your spine – don't tilt it back or tuck your chin. Imagining your chin is parallel to the floor will help. This is especially important when going uphill. Looking up the hill can strain your neck and make it hard to breathe.

- **Contract your abdominals.** With your spine tall, contract your stomach muscles slightly and lift them upwards to support your lower back. This will help you maintain your posture, as well as avoid straining your lower back.

- **Stabilize your hips.** Avoid swaying in your hips and placing undue pressure on your hips and knees by visualizing you have a full glass of water on each hip. As you walk, you need to extend up through the spine, contract your abdominals and keep those glasses of water full. This is an essential little tip if you want to get a firmer, flatter tummy but also a necessity if you have had any hip or knee surgery. It will significantly reduce pressure through your joints and you will instantly look better.

Case Study

Dorothy came on one of my four-day walking courses. She was carrying excess weight and walked with a stick as her knees were tender and sore. Walking with a stick gave her confidence, and she felt it reduced the pressure on her knees. One of the technique tips that made a massive difference to Dorothy was the full glasses of water exercise (see above). In fact, it made such a difference to her walking stride that after a day she was no longer swaying to lean on the stick to take the pressure off her knees. After day two, she left her stick in her room and walked without it; and on days three and four she was walking relatively smoothly and with good technique around the grounds. At the end of the course she left looking like a completely different person, just by visualizing the glasses of water and keeping them full as she walked.

Find the Right Pace for You

Now that you have the technique, you're ready to pick up the pace – how fast you walk – and find the right pace for you. A good pace varies depending on your fitness level, walking technique, and even walking location.

Your pace will affect your breathing. The faster you walk, the harder you'll breathe. Walking at a brisk pace can give you the same aerobic benefits as jogging.

- **Maintain a brisk pace.** You want to walk briskly – the way you would if you were late for an appointment or hurrying to catch a bus. You should be able to walk and talk at the same time, but this should be a breathy conversation and not a monologue or gossip!
- **Breathe freely.** Your pace should increase your breathing rate, even to the point where you're slightly winded. However, you're overexerting yourself if you can't talk and are completely out of breath.

To help you expend energy and streamline your hips and thighs, you need to find your optimum walking pace. This is easy to do, and once you have mastered it your body will definitely reap the rewards. Here's what you do:

Find Your Break Point

Your break point is your walking pace at which you are walking so fast you are just about to break into a jog. While I do not recommend that you walk for long periods at your break point, it is useful to help you find your optimum walking pace.

To find your walking break point, go somewhere with plenty of room, such as a park, country path, open land or quiet wide pavement. You will find it hard to complete this drill effectively if you have to dodge in and out of other people! Start walking, remember your technique and gradually pick up your speed. Swinging your arms faster will help you increase your stride speed. Continue to increase your walking pace, being strict with yourself to maintain a walking stride until you feel you cannot maintain a walk any longer, and you need to break into a jog. The point where you break into a jog is your break point. From your break point, drop back to your walking pace by 3–5 per cent – this is now your optimum walking pace. You should feel like you are walking with a purpose, and at a much faster pace than normal. On your first few walking outings on your six-week plan, I suggest you do this break point drill several times to help you become familiar with your optimum pace. You can check your optimum walking pace with a 'talking test'. If you are walking slowly enough to carry a tune you are probably walking too slowly. If you're gasping for air, slow down.

Speed up, Slow Down

A good way to increase your pace, improve your endurance and familiarize yourself with your break point is to pick up the pace for short spells in between your steady pace. This is often referred to as interval training. After you've been walking comfortably for about five minutes, increase your speed for a minute or two, then return to your steady pace. Working your way up to a brief but high-intensity walk can keep your walking routine challenging and help you improve your fitness level.

Establish Your Baseline Number of Steps

Establishing your baseline number of steps is important before you start your walking plan. It will help you choose the correct walking programme for you, and it will also give you a benchmark of your existing activity levels. You can find out how to establish your baseline number of steps on pages 125 and 129.

Invest in a Comfortable Pair of Shoes

You don't have to spend a fortune on walking shoes, but you do need a pair that provides you with support and won't rub.

Ten Tips for Finding Walking Shoes that Fit

- **Buy the right size.** Don't choose shoes by the size marked inside. Go by how they feel on your feet. Sizes can vary by style and brand.
- **Match shoes to the shape of your foot.** Choose shoes that fit as closely as possible.
- **Take the wiggle test.** The toe box of the shoes should be roomy enough for you to wiggle your toes freely and without pressure – but not so loose that your feet slide around in the shoes.
- **Buy shoes at the end of the day.** The longer you're on your feet, the more they swell. Most people's feet are largest at the end of the day, so it's important to fit and buy your shoes then.
- **Bring innerwear.** Try on shoes with socks or any special inserts you would normally wear.
- **Allow a space of three-eighths to half an inch from the tip of your longest toe to the tip of the shoes.** If you can push the tip of your index finger between the tip of your longest toe and the end of the shoes, the shoe length is OK.
- **Make sure the widest part of your feet fit comfortably in the wide part of the shoes when standing.** One trick is to stand and ask a friend to draw the shape of your feet on a piece of paper. Take the paper with you when you buy your shoes and make sure the shoes you're considering cover the drawing completely.
- **Don't expect shoes to 'stretch out'.** If the shoes feel too tight, don't buy them. With time, your feet may push or stretch shoes to fit, but this can cause foot pain and damage and should be avoided.
- **Avoid slipping.** Make sure your heels aren't slipping around in the shoes.
- **Take a walk.** Before you buy them, put both shoes on and walk around the store. Make sure they fit and feel good.

Walk with a friend or family member, or take the dog for a walk. Companionship helps you stay motivated. There have been anecdoctal reports that walking with your partner and sharing time together can boost your relationship, and there have even been cases where walking has saved relationships.

The Eating Plan

The eating plan is designed around a daily intake of 1,400–1,700 calories. This has been shown to be effective – in conjunction with exercise – in achieving a 6 per cent weight loss and stabilizing glucose levels in type 2 diabetes. This is a realistic amount of weight to lose, and it will have a major, positive impact on your health.

The plan contains plenty of fruits, vegetables, whole grains, low-fat dairy products and small amounts of lean meat and fish and applies the principles of a low-to-moderate glycaemic eating plan. It is also low in sodium, and follows the findings of the acclaimed DASH (Dietary Approaches to Stop Hypertension) study published in the *Journal of the American Medical Association* in 2003. This showed that a low-salt diet is effective in lowering blood pressure, which may consequently reduce the risk of cardiovascular disease and stroke.

The eating plan focuses on three main themes:

- Carb Curfew
- Calorie restriction through optimum nutrition
- GI principles

Carb Curfew – the Effective Calorie Controller

My highly effective Carb Curfew plan means no bread, pasta, rice, potatoes or cereal after 5pm. It is an effective way to cut down your calories as well as to achieve a better balance of nutrients, especially from fruit and vegetables. You can still get your essential whole-grain carbohydrates for breakfast and lunch, but you avoid them in your evening meal. This approach is simple to follow, and to help you there are menu plans in Chapter 7 and plenty of delicious Carb Curfew recipes in Chapter 8.

There is mounting evidence that decreasing the amount of processed carbohydrates we consume can have a positive effect on our health, reducing abdominal fat and middle-age spread and lowering blood glucose levels. Following my Carb Curfew will give you some great benefits, which I have described below.

Benefit 1: Reduces Bloating

Operating Carb Curfew and omitting carbohydrates from your evening meal will help reduce bloating, improve digestion, increase energy levels and can assist a better night's sleep. These benefits can be felt almost immediately.

When food is digested and broken down by the body, excessive amounts of glucose get stored as glycogen. This is important as a source of fuel for our muscles. However, as we have seen (see page 30), we already have a significant amount of stored body fat and glycogen in the muscles. To store one unit of glycogen, your body requires three units of water. If you imagine that each unit of glycogen is an orange and each water unit is an apple, each glycogen unit gets packed with three water units – that's one orange and three apples for each unit of glycogen your body needs to store. Cutting out carbohydrates in the evening means there is less glycogen to store and therefore less of a problem with bloating.

Benefit 2: Boosts Vital Fruit and Vegetable Intake

By following my Carb Curfew, you'll find it much easier to boost your intake of fruits and vegetables. Studies have shown that fruit and vegetable consumption in the UK is far below what it should be, with the average person eating fewer than three pieces a day, way below the recommended 'five a day', and a far cry from the five to nine pieces encouraged by leading anti-cancer organizations. However, fruit and vegetable consumption is worse among younger age groups; people over 50 are consuming more – so you should enjoy the extra fruit and vegetable ideas in this book.

Calorie Restriction through Optimum Nutrition

On your six-week eating plan you will be consuming fewer calories. However, this is not a deprivation diet, such as ones you may have experienced in the past. The key to this plan is to cut the calories but maintain the optimum nutritional content of your daily food intake.

Extensive research studies have shown that calorie restriction without undernutrition is remarkably beneficial in extending lifespan. Animals placed on low-calorie, optimal diets have shown a slowing of the typical signs of ageing, such as the usual decline in immune function or loss of functional capacity. This approach has also been found to reduce the risk of kidney disease, autoimmune diseases, diabetes and a variety of neurodegenerative diseases such as stroke, Parkinson's disease, Alzheimer's disease and Huntington's chorea. While most of this evidence to date has been shown in animal studies, there is some human evidence from the population of the Japanese island of Okinawa.

The People of Okinawa

Newsweek magazine featured a story about the high percentage of centenarians – individuals aged 100 or older – who reside on the island of Okinawa in Japan. Researchers were fascinated to learn that of the island's 1.3 million residents, approximately 600 had reached their 100th birthday. This startling ratio makes Okinawa home to the highest proportion of centenarians in the world: 39.5 for every 100,000 people compared to about 10 in 100,000 in the UK and US. Investigations into the Okinawa way of life revealed that most islanders consume a high-quality diet consisting mainly of home-grown vegetables, tofu and seaweed. They also tend to live low-stress, physically active lives. But what sparked the most attention was the fact that while most Okinawans have protein and fat intakes similar to those of their fellow citizens, their calorie levels are 20 per cent lower than the Japanese national average.

Suddenly switching to a diet of seaweed and tofu may seem a massive jump, a far cry from my concept of taking small steps for big change. However, if you look at it from a calorie perspective, a 20 per cent decrease in your existing intake is not that much. If you are consuming, on average, 2,100 calories a day, your intake according to the Okinawa example would be 1,680. The key issue is consistency, and making your lower calorie intake nutritionally dense and satisfying. Following the six-week eating plan will make this process easy for you.

The Biosphere Study

An experiment in Tucson, Arizona, inadvertently provided further evidence of the health benefits of calorie restriction. In this study, the research participants lived in a self-contained ecological space, and were reduced to eating a low-calorie diet after experiencing unanticipated problems with their crop cultivation. The original intention of the study was for the participants to eat 2,500 calories per day. However, they actually ended up averaging only 1,800 calories a day for their first six months, then switched to about 2,000 calories daily for the remaining 18 months. At the end of this unplanned diet the male participants had lost 18 per cent of their body weight while the women had shed 10 per cent. Their diet consisted primarily of vegetables, fruits, nuts, grains and legumes, supplemented with modest amounts of dairy, eggs and meat. From a health perspective, at the end of the two years, participants had not only lost weight but also reduced their blood pressure, blood glucose, insulin, total cholesterol, low-density lipoprotein (LDL) and triglyceride levels, all of which, when elevated, are linked to the development of long-term disease.

The key to reducing calories successfully is to retain a sufficient amount of micronutrients, protein and essential fats in daily meal planning. The six-week menu plan and recipes have taken care of this for you. Your eating plan is NOT a diet, in the conventional sense of the word, nor does it involve arbitrarily excluding calories. Instead, it should be undertaken as a lifestyle change in terms of what you eat and how you move. You are doing this not just to lose weight and to look good but also to retard ageing, prevent disease and enhance your health, energy, mobility and wellbeing.

So, you might ask, why can't I just restrict my calories to lose weight? Surely the weight will just drop off? This may sound a bit drastic, but if you restrict your calories without eating adequate nutrients, deficiencies will result similar to those seen in undernourished populations or people with eating disorders. These deficiencies can include an increased incidence of infection and depression of the immune system, lack of stature in adults and lower steroid levels. While difficulty with lactation in breastfeeding mothers may not be of particular concern at this stage of your life, a decrease in your bone density and osteoporosis are most definitely matters of serious concern. Yes, you may want to lose weight, but improvements in your health are of equal importance.

Calorie Restriction and the Ageing Process

The exact mechanism of how optimum nutrition with calorie restriction enhances health is still being unravelled. It is known that effective, sustainable, healthy weight loss has a direct effect on your risk of heart disease. Weight loss reduces levels of triglycerides, total cholesterol and unhealthy LDL cholesterol, all of which are associated with an elevated risk of heart disease.

There are two main schools of thought about how optimum nutrition and calorie restriction inhibit the ageing process. One relates to the cumulative effect of oxidative damage, and the other to our resistance to insulin.

Ageing and Oxidative Damage

Some experts have attributed the signs and symptoms of ageing to the effects of 'free radicals' on the body. Normal energy metabolism, in which food is converted to energy by the body, produces these harmful free radicals. It is thought that when calorie consumption is restricted, the body's metabolism or its 'rate of living' gradually declines due to the decrease in these free radicals. This reduces the level of oxidative damage to the cells, and the signs and symptoms of ageing are believed to be diminished.

This, however, has yet to be clinically proven in humans, although studies involving rodents have shown declines in oxidative damage when calories are restricted. There is also evidence that calorie restriction can enhance the body's immune system, boosting its defences against damage.

Ageing and Insulin Levels

This second theory is relatively new. Insulin helps regulate the composition of our cell walls as well as creating an optimum environment for maintaining and caring for our tissues. When these growth factors are disturbed, the kind of cells proliferate that are commonly seen with cancer and atherosclerosis ('furring up' of the artery walls). As we age, levels of growth hormone tend to diminish, and the cell membrane composition deteriorates. Growth hormone levels and cell membrane composition are both indirectly affected by exposure to insulin after we consume a large meal. When calories are restricted, insulin exposure is lowered. Some scientists have suggested that calorie restriction may help to moderate insulin levels over a person's lifetime, thereby decreasing the risk of disease.

How this Affects Weight

There is no doubt that the whole ageing process is exacerbated by carrying excess weight. Too much body fat is associated with insulin resistance, high blood pressure, high total and unhealthy LDL cholesterol, diabetes and coronary heart disease. Visceral fat is of particular concern. This is the type of fat that accumulates around the midriff, perhaps lovingly referred to as a 'spare tyre'. This middle-age spread, however, is also lodged deeply around your internal organs. As we age, this visceral fat tends to increase internally, upping the risk of atherosclerosis and insulin resistance.

Putting Optimum Nutrition Calorie Restriction into Practice

To be honest, even if you are committed to improving your health and shedding excess weight for good, it can be difficult to alter lifelong habits. Regularly eating too many calories or leading a fairly sedentary life can be difficult patterns to break. But the good news is that by applying the concept of small steps for big change, you can make a huge and lasting impact to your body, well-being and appearance. Although beneficial at any age, moving towards a lighter diet and leaner body can be especially important as we grow older. Studies have found that being overweight in middle age (35–45) can cut as much as three years off your life expectancy; and being overweight at 50 can cut your life expectancy by eight to ten years.

Glycaemic Index Eating Principles

The glycaemic index (GI) ranks carbohydrate foods based on how quickly the carbohydrates enter the bloodstream and elevate blood sugar levels. Technically speaking, the GI of a certain food is determined by comparing the blood glucose-raising effects of 50 grams of carbohydrate from a particular carbohydrate food to the blood glucose-raising effects of 50g of glucose (considered to be the standard) over a specific period of time. Recently glycaemic index foods and following a GI diet have become a key issue for health and weight management, as it is believed that following a low-to-moderate GI diet helps stabilize blood sugar levels, keeps hunger at bay and reduces the storage of fat through elevated insulin. However, what has been lost in the GI craze is that a number of important factors can affect the GI rating of a food and the classification of a food as simply high, medium or low GI is not necessarily strictly accurate. By following the GI Walking Diet eating plan and the concept of

Carb Curfew, you will be automatically be following a more GI style of eating, and you'll notice an improvement in your energy levels as well as optimizing a healthier weight for you.

How GI Works

The glycaemic index focuses on how rapidly a carbohydrate is absorbed from your small intestine into your blood and how rapidly this raises insulin levels. A dramatic rise in insulin levels in the blood causes two responses:

- ◆ the removal of carbohydrate as a panic response to flooding and thus a lowering of the blood sugar beyond normal (hypoglycaemia)
- ◆ an increase in fat storage

The quicker carbohydrates leave the small intestine and flood the blood, the more insulin responds and also floods the blood. You may have experienced this yourself, perhaps when you reached to eat something sweet as you felt lethargic and needed a sugar fix or boost of energy. Thirty minutes later you felt more tired than before you had eaten your sugar fix, due to the hypoglycaemic backlash response. This may also trigger feeding and make you eat even more, which may not necessarily be good for weight management.

The test to determine the GI of a particular food is to eat 50 grams of carbohydrate from the food in question and then to have your blood glucose levels monitored for two hours. The level of blood glucose and the speed at which it rises are then compared with the figures when 50 grams of pure glucose are consumed. The faster your digestive system breaks down the carbohydrate, the quicker it will leave the small intestine and enter the blood and the higher the rating it is given compared to glucose, which is rated 100.

Good GI Foods

In general non-starchy vegetables, fruits, legumes and nuts usually have a low GI. A low GI rating implies that the effect of a low GI food will be to raise your blood sugar quite slowly. This has the effect of helping to stabilize blood sugar levels and reduce hunger. Many factors affect the GI value of a particular food, including its variety, whether it was processed and how it was prepared. For example, there are many varieties of rice, each with its own type of starch. In the case of a boiled potato the GI can be increased by as much as 25 per cent if it is mashed as opposed to served in small matchbox-sized cubes. Even subtle differences in the ripeness of a banana can double its GI.

The following table provides a list of some of broad categories of GI foods. However, by following the GI Walking Diet eating plan and using the delicious recipes in Chapter 8 you will automatically be applying the broad principles of GI, making it simple and easy to follow.

Glycaemic Index of Various Foods

High GI Foods (GI > 85)	Moderate GI Foods (GI = 60–85)	Low GI Foods (GI < 60)
Angel Food Cake	Sponge Cake	Ironman Bar (chocolate)
Boiled Sweets	Corn Tortilla	Milk (whole/skimmed)
Ice Cream	Green Peas	9-Grain Bread
Honey/Syrups	Grapes, Bananas	Tomato Soup/Juice
Corn Chips	White Rice (long grain)	Yogurt (all types)
Mashed Potatoes	Pastry	Grapefruit/Oranges
Croissants, Doughnuts	Pitta Bread (white)	Rice Bran, Brown Rice
Coca Cola (Coke)	Bran Chex Cereal	Apple (whole/juice)
Raisins, Watermelon	Oatmeal (cooked)	Peaches, Pears (fresh)
Cheerios, Cornflakes	Orange/Grapefruit juice	Beans (all types)
Cream of Wheat	Snickers Bar	Peanuts/Cashews
Sport Drinks	PowerBar (chocolate)	All Bran Cereal
English Muffins	Oat Bran Cereal	
Waffles, Pancakes	Ice Cream, low fat	
White Bread, Bagels,	Durum Spaghetti	
Corn Bran Cereal	Oat Bran Bread	
Soda Crackers	7-Grain Bread	
Total Cereal	Special K Cereal	
Pop Tarts	Sweet Corn	
Grapenuts	100% Wholemeal Bread	
Rice Krispies		
Shredded Wheat		

Interestingly, researchers at Children's Hospital Boston and Brigham and Women's Hospital in Boston tracked 39 dieters until they had lost 20 pounds apiece. The dieters followed either a low-glyacemic or a low-fat plan: both provided 1,500 calories a day. The low-glycemic group lost the weight a bit faster than the low-fat group, but – more to the point – the low-glycaemic dieters maintained a faster metabolic rate, burning about 80 more calories daily.

Following a low-to-moderate GI diet is not the only way to successful weight management and a healthy and optimum weight loss, but when you combine the three principles of Carb Curfew, calorie restriction through optimum nutrition and a GI eating plan, you are on to a winner for your taste buds, your health *and* your waist line!

The Menu Plans

The meal options include vegetarian dishes, traditional favourites and foods we enjoy on a regular basis. Foods that you may have considered forbidden have been given a healthy and delicious makeover. Plus there are recipes incorporating essential ingredients for your health, so whether you suffer from arthritis, osteoporosis or diabetes, you can eat enjoyably and healthily. All are high in taste, flavour and texture but low in sodium. All fulfil the six-week plan criteria, helping you to achieve a weight loss of 6 per cent without deprivation or putting your life on hold. So whether you love to entertain, cater for a large family, live alone or just can't live without your Sunday roast, you'll find you don't have to miss out.

Putting the eating plan into operation couldn't be easier. There are two approaches to choose from.

The Six-week Eating Plan

This is the more structured approach, and offers you daily menus. All you have to do is follow the plans, check out the recipes and enjoy the food. The daily plans have taken care of all the important criteria you need to have in place to make the plan work for you.

You'll find the full six-week daily menu plans on pages 197–209. Each daily plan is based on three meals and one snack, a daily calorie intake of 1,400–1,700. Low in sodium, the diet contains plenty of fruits, vegetables, whole grains, low-fat dairy products and lean meat and fish.

If you like, you can mix and match your menu plans, and you can swap some of the dishes around, as you will soon discover your personal favourites.

The Flexible Eating Plan

Alternatively, you may prefer to follow a more flexible approach to your diet during the six-week plan. You can devise your own menu plans by selecting from the lists of breakfasts, lunches, dinners and snacks. Each option is calorie-counted, the ideas are comprehensive and the recipes are easy to follow and to cook.

Each meal idea has been calorie-counted and nutritionally analysed for you. If you want to put together your own menu plans, I suggest you follow these daily calorie breakdowns. If following a 1,400-calorie menu plan, it is advisable for you to divide your calories up through the day as follows:

Breakfast: 350
Lunch: 400
Dinner: 450
Snack: 200

If following more of a 1,700 daily calorie allowance, I suggest you divide your calories up as follows:

Breakfast: 400
Lunch: 500
Dinner: 600
Snack: 200

Spreading your calories out like this will help stabilize your blood sugar levels and ensure you are not consuming all your calories at the end of the day, a strategy that's been shown to aggravate cravings and weight gain.

Now that you have seen how the six-week plan works, let's get you ready to start.

5 Getting Ready for Action

Everyone should take their dog for a walk
every day – even if they don't have one.

So you've read all about the impact of ageing on your body, how middle-age spread is real, and how the GI Walking Diet is going to help you achieve results. But what condition is your body in at the start of your six-week plan? In this chapter you can establish exactly where you are before you embark on getting healthier and losing weight. This is important not just to get you motivated but also to allow you to set a bench mark.

You won't achieve your weight loss or health improvement goals overnight. That isn't realistic. You need to invest time in your efforts, and your body has to adapt to all the great health investments you are making.

Let's start by doing a Five-minute Body Road Test to establish some facts and figures about your body.

Your Five-minute Body Road Test

Complete this quiz to see if you need to do the six-week plan.

Circle the number that answers each question best for you. Then add up your score at the end of each section.

Nutrition

How many days a week do you eat at least three pieces of fruit?

Seven: 4
Five to six: 3
Three to four: 2
Two to three: 1
None: 0

How many days a week do you eat a meal which includes vegetables?

Seven: 4
Five to six: 3
Three to four: 2
One to two: 1
None: 0

How do you spread butter or margarine on your bread?

Don't have it: 2
Thickly: 0
Thinly: 1

How often do you eat fatty foods such as pies, pastries, sausage rolls?

Seldom or never: (3)

Once or twice a week: 2

Three or four times a week: 1

Daily or almost daily: 0

How often do you eat fish?

Daily or almost daily: 3

Three or four times a week: 2

Once or twice a week: (1)

Seldom or never: 0

How many different colours of fruits and vegetables do you have on your plate at any one time?

Three: 3

Two: (2)

One: 1

None, I only eat potatoes: 0

Nutrition Score

17–19: You are doing well. Keep up the healthy diet. You'll find more exciting, tasty and healthy recipes and menu plans in Chapters 7 and 8.

11–16: There is definitely room for improvement here. But don't worry – it doesn't have to be that difficult. You'll find lots of ways to boost your nutrient intake in Chapter 7.

0–10: You need help. Have a look at the recipes and menu plans in Chapters 7 and 8. Don't panic – start slowly and enjoy the process. Remember, small steps make big changes, and you'll find lots of helpful tips in this book.

Physical Activity

Over the past seven days, how many times have you done physical activity that got you hot and sweaty?

None: 0

One to two: 1

Three to four: 2

Five to six: 3

More than seven: 4

How long does each bout of physical activity last?

30 minutes or more: 3

15–30 minutes: 2

Up to 15 minutes: 1

I don't exercise at all: 0

How many hours do you sit each day? (include home, leisure activities and work)

Zero to eight hours: 2

Eight to twelve hours: 1

Twelve or more hours: 0

How often do you drive the car when you could walk?

Daily or almost daily: 0

Three or four times a week: 1

Once or twice a week: 2

Seldom or never: 3

How often do you take a walk, either alone or with your family, a dog or friends?

Daily or almost daily: 3

Three or four times a week: 2

Once or twice a week: 1

Seldom or never: 0

Do you struggle to open tight jars, unbutton a shirt or pick up small objects?

Seldom or never: 3

Once or twice a week: 2

Three or four times a week: 1

Daily or almost daily: 0

Do you find it difficult to get out of a low chair or to balance on one leg?

Seldom or never: 3

Once or twice a week: 2

Three or four times a week: 1

Daily or almost daily: 0

Physical Activity Score

17–21: Well done – you obviously enjoy your physical activity. Remember, the most important investment you can make is to provide your body with a rounded fitness programme. This includes cardiovascular activity together with strength and mobility exercises. Following the GI Walking Diet will keep you fit, improve your health and provide that great long-term health investment.

11–16: There is room for a little improvement. Physical activity is imperative as we get older. Remember, it becomes more about strength and balance as well as the huff and puff of our heart and lungs.

0–10: Getting physically active may seem daunting but inactivity is a fast-track to ageing and accelerates the loss of physical independence. Taking small steps now need not be painful or too time-consuming, and the rewards can be significant. Go on – make that start.

The Check-up

When was the last time you had a check-up with your doctor?
Within the last year: 4
One or two years ago: 3
Three or four years ago: 2
More than four years ago: 1
Never: 0

Do you know the result of your last cholesterol test?
Yes: 1
No/Haven't had one done: 0

Do you know the result of your last blood pressure check?
Yes: 1
No/Haven't had one done: 0

Do you know the result of your last blood glucose check?
Yes: 1
No/Haven't had one done: 0

Do you know whether or not you are in the healthy weight range?
Yes: 1
No: 0

Do you know your waist circumference?

Yes: 1

No: 0

Do you know your body mass index?

Yes: 1

No: 0

The Check-up Score

8–10: You obviously know a lot about your physical health – so let's take action and start the GI Walking Diet to make the best possible health investment!

5–7: If you have any concerns about your health, have a chat with your GP before you start the GI Walking Diet. Then make an appointment six weeks later and see how impressed they'll be.

0–4: Establishing some important medical information would be a good idea. Knowing what shape you are in now can help you identify any potential problems and give you a bench mark to see how you can improve after following the GI Walking Diet.

Establishing Body Facts

As you age, you need to be aware of some facts and figures about your body, particularly in later life. These figures give you an insight into your state of health. You can easily establish these facts by yourself or with your GP's help. Knowing these statistics at the start of your Walking Plan will give you a bench mark for your health. As you progress through the six-week plan, you will be able to see how your efforts are positively impacting your health and well-being. Knowing these body facts can also serve as a great motivator, spurring you on when your enthusiasm may start to fade a little. So what are the body facts and figures you should know?

Waistline Circumference

What it Means

Waistline circumference, as it suggests, is the measurement around your waist. It reflects abdominal obesity, the fat deposited around the abdominal organs.

The Healthy Range

People are considered to be at an increased health risk if they have the following waist measurements:
  ◆ Men: more than 94cm/37 inches
  ◆ Women: more than 80cm/31 inches

People are thought to be at a substantially increased health risk if their waist measures:

- Men: more than 102cm/40 inches
- Women: more than 88cm/35 inches   36½

Why You Need to Care

Excessive waistlines are associated with an increased risk of heart disease and diabetes. Recent evidence suggests that waist circumference on its own indicates not only the amount of abdominal fat you have but also total body fat. People's waistlines have expanded significantly over the past 10–20 years. If your waist circumference is more than 94cm (men) or 80cm (women), any further weight gain increases the risk of metabolic complications, such as diabetes, elevated blood fat levels and glucose sensitivity. And if your waist circumference is above 102cm (men) or 88cm (women), you need to take action now and reduce your weight, because there is a substantial risk of metabolic complications.

> When you measure your waist, make sure your tape measure is flat. The waist is the smallest part of the abdomen. For some, this may be level with the belly button but for others it may be slightly higher.

What You Can Do

Following the six-week exercise plan will help you lose weight and, more importantly, inches off your waistline. In a study, 30 obese males who followed an exercise programme for four months without adjusting their diet decreased their waist circumference by an average of nearly 14 per cent. Following the eating plan is also important, however, as it has been designed to be low in trans fats, which have been shown to increase waist circumference.

Blood Cholesterol Level

What it Means

Your blood cholesterol level is the amount of fat in your blood. A simple blood test is done after you fast for nine to twelve hours. It is advisable to take the test every five years starting at the age of 20.

The Healthy Range

Total cholesterol should be below 200 milligrams per decilitre (mg/dl). HDL or 'good' cholesterol should be above 40mg/dl. LDL or 'bad' cholesterol should be less than 130mg/dl. Triglycerides should be less than 150mg/dl.

Why You Need to Care

High cholesterol levels are a major risk factor for heart attack and stroke. Lowering total cholesterol levels by just 10 per cent may reduce the incidence of heart disease by about 30 per cent, according to the Center for Disease Control in the US.

What You Can Do

Following the GI Walking Diet will help keep your cholesterol levels in check. Try to eat a low-fat diet. When choosing meat, stick mostly to chicken and fish, which are lower in cholesterol than beef and lamb. You should limit your intake of saturated fats – found mainly in meats, whole milk, whole-milk products and coconuts – since these raise your cholesterol levels. Trans fats found in packaged foods – including cakes and biscuits, some cereals, frozen meals, hard margarine and fried fast foods – are as harmful as saturated fats, if not more so. They raise levels of harmful low-density lipoprotein (LDL) cholesterol and lower the good, high-density lipoprotein (HDL) cholesterol. You can find out more about trans fats on page 179.

Don't forget the importance of walking. Regular physical exercise – roughly 30 minutes every day – is one of the most effective ways in which you can control your cholesterol levels. Daily physical activity improves your cholesterol profile, lowering bad LDL cholesterol and raising good HDL cholesterol.

Body Mass Index (BMI)

What it Means

BMI is the ratio of a person's weight to height, and is now the most widely used measure to classify underweight, overweight and obesity in adults. Measuring your weight in relation to your height is thought to be a good indicator of how much body fat you have. A person's body mass is comprised of two main components:

Lean body mass (LBM) – lean muscle and the vital organs. In fact, everything that is not fat.

Body fat mass (BFM) – the total amount of adipose (fat) tissue in the body.

Your BMI is calculated by dividing your weight in kilos by the square of your height in metres – kg/m². If you don't fancy doing the arithmetic you can log on to my website www.joannahall.com and it will calculate your BMI automatically for you.

The Healthy Range

BMI is broken down into five broad categories:

Category	BMI Value (kg/m²)	Health Risks
Underweight	less than 18.5	Low but other risks increased★
Normal	18.5–24.9	Average
Overweight	25.0–29.9	Increased
Obese	30.0–34.9	Moderate
Morbidly obese	more than 35.0	Severe

27.1809

★ Risks of being underweight include decreased fertility, amenorrhoea (abnormal absence of menstruation), and a potential reduction in bone density.

Why You Need to Care

A BMI above 30 indicates too much body fat. Carrying too much weight puts you at higher risk for a variety of conditions including diabetes, heart disease, stroke, high blood pressure, osteoarthritis and breathing problems. You also increase your risk of some forms of cancer (specifically uterine, kidney, gall bladder, colorectal and breast). In fact, women in the Harvard Nurses' Health Study who gained more than 44 pounds after the age of 18 doubled their risk of breast cancer compared to women whose weight remained the same.

However, it is important to note that under some circumstances it may not be appropriate to rely on a BMI measurement. This is because BMI doesn't distinguish between weight associated with fat and weight associated with muscle or water. For example, someone who is heavy and very muscular, such as an athlete, or someone who is suffering from oedema (fluid retention) may have a BMI above 30 but not excess body fat. It can also be difficult or impossible to measure the height and/or weight of someone who is unable to stand properly or who is bed-bound. BMI also gives no indication of where your body fat is distributed. This is important because it is not just the amount or the composition of excess weight that affects health, but also where the extra fat is stored within the body. Knowing your BMI is useful but it is particularly relevant when used in conjunction with your waist circumference measurement.

What You Can Do

If your BMI is too high, you need to lose weight by following the six-week exercise plan and eating plan. Reducing your BMI in conjunction with your waist circumference will have a positive effect on your health. If your BMI is too low, it is advisable for you to talk to a nutritionist or dietician about gaining some weight. Regular moderate physical activity is still important, however, as it will improve your health in other ways.

Blood Pressure

What it Means

Measures the amount of pressure your heart and blood vessels are under each time your heart pumps out blood. When you have your blood pressure taken, two numbers are recorded. The first (higher) number measures the pressure in your arteries when your heart contracts; and the second (lower) number indicates the pressure when your heart relaxes. Blood pressure should be checked at every doctor's appointment, or at least once a year, especially if you have a family history of high blood pressure.

The Healthy Range

Below 140/90 is considered healthy. However, some medication can distort your true blood pressure reading. Ask your GP about any drugs you may be taking that could affect your blood pressure.

Why You Need to Care

High blood pressure (hypertension) greatly increases your risk of stroke and heart attack. It can also harm your memory and coordination. A study in the *Hypertension* journal reported that elderly patients with moderate hypertension had slower reaction times and worse memory than those with normal blood pressure.

What You Can Do

Consume less than 2,400 milligrams of salt (about a teaspoon) each day and maintain a healthy weight through regular exercise. The DASH research study (*Journal of the American Medical Assocation*, 2003), on which the eating plan is based, found consumption of less than 1,500mg of sodium advisable and beneficial for health. Too much salt and being overweight can both raise blood pressure. Reduce your consumption of processed foods such as canned soups and frozen ready meals, since these are often high in sodium. Increase your intake of vegetables, which are naturally high in potassium, a mineral that helps keep sodium levels in check. By following the six-week eating plan you will automatically keep your sodium levels low, and your intake of fruit and vegetables will naturally boost your potassium intake.

Daily Fat Intake

What it Means

Simply, this is the percentage of your daily calorie intake that comes from fat.

The Healthy Range

According to the British Dietetic Association, less than 30 per cent of your daily calorie intake should come from fat, with less than 10 per cent coming from saturated fats.

Why You Need to Care

If you are eating a lot of fat, it's likely that you are taking in extra calories, which leads to weight gain. Too much saturated fat will also raise your LDL (bad) cholesterol level, putting you at higher risk of heart disease. You may also be consuming too many harmful trans fats (see page 179).

What You Can Do

Consume monounsaturated and polyunsaturated fats (found in olive, canola, safflower and peanut oils, nuts and avocados), which help lower bad cholesterol. A study in the *American Journal of Clinical Nutrition* found that people with diets high in monounsaturated fats reduced their risk of heart disease by 21 per cent, while those who simply ate a low-fat diet reduced it by only 12 per cent. The six-week eating plan is naturally high in healthy monounsaturated fats, and low in unhealthy saturated fats.

Grip Strength

What it Means

Grip strength is literally the power of your hands. It is measured by holding a grip dynamometer and squeezing as hard as you can for about five seconds. You can have your grip strength measured at fitness and health clubs, or your GP's wellness centre may also offer this service.

The Healthy Range

The normal range is 20–30 kilograms, but the numbers often vary depending on your age and the device used.

Why You Need to Care

Poor grip strength and finger dexterity can have a direct impact on your day-to-day living. As well as making it difficult to perform simple tasks such as opening jars and stiff doors or buttoning clothes, several studies have shown that poor grip strength can indicate you are a candidate for osteoporosis. If yours is below average, talk to your doctor about your general risk for the disease.

What You Can Do

Make sure you get a good source of calcium from your diet each day. You'll find more information on calcium on page 190. By following the six-week menu plan you'll be taking care of your daily calcium needs. Weight-bearing exercises such as brisk walking and stair climbing, plus strength training in the six-week plan, can also help prevent osteoporosis. You can improve the strength of your forearms and hands by following the Get a Grip Programme, below.

Get a Grip Programme – Improve Your Hand Strength

Almost every action – from tying a shoelace and buttoning a shirt to driving a car – depends on the strength and agility of your hands, wrists and forearms. Yet they are constantly exposed to physical stress that can damage the nerves, tendons, muscles and soft tissues, and even lead to repetitive strain injury or carpal tunnel syndrome. Meanwhile, our growing reliance on push-button appliances can lead to a loss in grip strength and dexterity, which can become particularly problematic in later life.

The following exercises condition and strengthen the motor muscles of the hands, wrists and forearms to improve performance, protect against injury and ease daily tasks. They primarily target the wrist flexors and the small muscles of the fingers and hands, and are designed to take some of the workload off the wrist extensors, the muscles most likely to be affected by repetitive strain injury. These moves also reduce overall stiffness and promote finger dexterity and general mobility, so they are excellent for arthritis sufferers too. Practise any or all of them daily – or at least three times a week – and you'll soon be grabbing the benefits.

The Dexterity Test

Answer these few questions to establish your finger dexterity and strength.

- Can you play jacks and pick up the ball and a single jack without dropping them? YES/NO
- Can you open a tight-lidded jar? YES/NO
- Can you button and unbutton a shirt with one hand? YES/NO
- Can you touch your thumbs to each finger on the same hand quickly and without missing? YES/NO
- Can you flex your wrists to point your fingers straight down and straight up? YES/NO
- Can you move your hands efficiently along a computer keyboard without strain? YES/NO
- Can you easily do simple, small movements, such as threading a needle or picking up a pin dropped on the floor? YES/NO

If you answered 'no' to two or more questions, I'd strongly advise you to try the following conditioning exercises. They are easy to do – you definitely won't break into a sweat – but they can quickly improve your hand strength and finger dexterity. In fact, you'll notice a difference even after a week. If you have grandchildren, you'll find they also enjoy these exercises – why not let them be your personal trainer and take you through them? It's great for their coordination too.

Play Jacks

Sit comfortably at a table and toss a handful of jacks in front of you. At each bounce of the ball, pick up a jack with your right hand. Once you've picked up every jack, one at a time, progress to picking up two jacks per bounce, and so on until you can grab all 10 jacks in a single bounce. As you play, pay attention to your breathing pattern and the amount of effort it takes to scoop up the jacks. Begin again, and challenge your coordination by using your left hand to pick up the jacks.

- ◆ Benefit: Improves hand-eye coordination and finger dexterity.
- ◆ After a week: The game should get easier. Eventually you will be able to pick up all 10 jacks and grab the ball on a single bounce.

Finger Stretch

Hold your hands out in front of you with the fingers of each hand together, thumbs in towards the index fingers.

Stretch your fingers and thumbs as far apart as possible, then bring them together. Repeat opening and closing the digits 15–20 times.

- ◆ Benefit: Improves finger dexterity and range of motion.
- ◆ After a week: You should be able to spread your fingers wider and feel less tension in your hands.

Finger Push-ups

With fingers spread and elbows bent, press your hands firmly together, touching from the pads of the fingertips down to the palms.

Use the tension between the fingertips to arch the fingers out so that only the pads of the fingertips are touching.

Continue to press the fingers and thumbs together as you move them towards each other. Hold the tension as you close them. Repeat 15–20 times.

- ◆ Benefit: Improves finger and wrist strength.

- After a week: You can expect to open a jar more easily and grasp objects with a stronger grip.

Wrist Bend and Straighten

Hold your hands in front of you, arms and wrists straight, palms down. Bend both wrists, pointing your fingers towards the floor; hold this position for five counts. Straighten the wrists; repeat five times.

Reversing the direction, flex your wrists to point the fingers up; hold for five counts. Straighten your wrists; repeat five times.

- Benefit: Strengthens the wrists and forearms; helps relieve discomfort caused by carpal tunnel syndrome; a good wrist mobility exercise if you suffer from arthritic hands.
- After a week: Look for greater wrist flexibility and less tension in your forearms.

Towel Twister

Hold a rolled towel at chest height, arms straight and palms down, hands about shoulder-width apart. Pull the ends of the towel in opposite directions to create tension.

Keeping your arms straight and maintaining steady tension on the towel, twist the towel forwards, then backwards. Repeat 10–15 times.

- Benefit: Increases strength of hands and forearms, and wrist mobility.
- After a week: You should notice greater wrist flexibility and stronger forearms.

Prayer Pose

Press your palms together in front of your chest, fingers pointing up. Keeping the palms together, lift your elbows until you feel the stretch in your forearms. Hold for 10–15 seconds.

Reverse the action: Place the backs of your hands together with the fingers pointing down. Lower the elbows and hold for 10–15 seconds.

- ◆ Benefit: Strengthens the wrists and hands.
- ◆ After a week: You will feel less strain and more flexibility in the wrists, along with greater forearm strength.

More Handy Moves

Try these extra exercises. You'll be surprised how simple yet challenging they can be.

- ◆ **Flipovers**. Lay your forearm on a table, palm down. Keeping your little finger on the table, turn your hand so the palm faces up. Return to starting position and repeat 5–10 times. Switch hands, then repeat. For a greater challenge, hold a 0.5–1.5kg (1 to 3 pound) weight.
  - ➤ Benefit: Strengthens the forearm rotators that allow you to turn your palms up and down.
- ◆ **Drumming**. Place just your fingers on a tabletop with your lowest knuckle at the edge of the table and your entire palm off the table. Keeping your wrist straight and palms still, use only your fingers to 'drum' on the table. Experiment by moving your fingers far apart then together, and drumming fast then slow.
  - ➤ Benefit: Improves finger dexterity; strengthens wrist muscles.
- ◆ **Making O's**. Place your elbows on a table, forearms at 90 degrees to the table, keeping wrists straight. Lightly touch each thumb to each fingertip on its respective hand, forming an 'O', then straighten and spread the fingers after each O. Repeat 15–20 times, increasing the speed. You can make this exercise more fun for younger family members by placing finger puppets on each finger and making up stories.
  - ➤ Benefit: Improves finger dexterity and hand–eye coordination.

- **Fine Fists.** Hold your hands out in front of you, elbows bent and palms facing in. Gradually make a fist by first bending the joint closest to the tip of each finger, then bending the middle joint and so on, until the fingertips touch the palm. Unfold to starting position, reversing the process. Repeat 5–10 times.
  - ➤ Benefit: Improves hand function and mobility.
- **Hangover.** Holding a 0.5–1.5kg (1 to 3 pound) dumbbell, lay your forearm on a table with your wrist straight, facing up, and hanging past the edge of the table. Flex your wrist upwards, lifting the dumbbell. Lower and repeat 10–15 times, then switch hands and repeat.
  - ➤ Benefit: Strengthens wrist flexors.
- **Ball Squeezes.** Holding a squishy ball firmly in your palm, squeeze and release tension on the ball 10–15 times.
  - ➤ Benefit: Strengthens hands, wrists and forearms.

Thyroid Level

What it Means

This is the level of thyroid-stimulating hormone (TSH) your pituitary gland produces. A simple blood test can tell if your thyroid is overactive, which is called hyperthyroidism, or underactive, which is called hypothyroidism.

The Healthy Range
A normal amount of TSH is 0.4 to 5 milli-international units per litre (miU/L).

Why You Need to Care

It is thought that many people suffer from a thyroid disorder, but more than half are undiagnosed. About one out of every eight women will develop a thyroid problem at some point in her life, and women are five to eight times more likely to have the condition than men. Symptoms of hypothyroidism include sluggishness, weight gain, depression and heavy menstrual periods. Hyperthyroidism typically results in excessive weight loss, sweating, anxiety and an elevated heart rate.

What You Can Do

While you cannot prevent a thyroid condition, the best way to protect your health is to keep tabs on your TSH level so you can get treatment if a problem develops. It is advisable to be tested every five years from the age of 35, but get screened earlier and annually if you have a family history of thyroid disorders. People often blame their weight problems on thyroid disorders. They may feel any attempts to lose weight are doomed to failure. However, as the following case history shows, a thyroid condition is not a valid excuse for abandoning exercise and healthy eating.

Case Study

Mary had struggled with her weight since her early 40s, and a lot of the excess weight had accumulated around her middle. Now in her early 50s, she had tried many weight-loss products, clubs and approaches, but had been frustrated by her lack of success. A professional caterer, she acknowledged it was easy for her to snack on tasty nibbles and turn a blind eye to what she was doing. When Mary's doctor diagnosed her with an underactive thyroid, she felt that her efforts to lose weight would always be in vain. She decided not to bother – what was the point? I started Mary on a walking programme, asking her to complete walks on five out of seven days each week for both accumulating steps and intensity. In addition, I asked her to operate my Carb Curfew and to monitor her weight every week. After six weeks she had lost 7 pounds, which was a real success for her, and after 10 weeks she had lost 12 pounds. Three months later, she had gone on to lose a further 8 pounds, giving her a total weight loss of 20 pounds, an amount she never thought possible because of her thyroid problem.

Testing Your Fitness

In Chapter 1, we identified the components that are vitally important for our fitness and wellbeing:

- Strength
- Endurance
- Flexibility
- Mobility

The following simple tests measure your body's performance in each of these areas. Each will be improved when you follow the six-week exercise plan. Do these tests before you begin the plan and as soon as you have finished. They are quick to do, and establish a performance bench mark for you to monitor your progress against.

In my experience, many clients can be a little reluctant to do these simple tests at the beginning. Sometimes there is a fear that their score will be low; they may feel embarrassed; or they may just be impatient to get going. Clients who don't do the tests before they complete the six-week plan always regret it. They feel so much better and fitter afterwards, and are annoyed not to have any base measurements against which to compare their improvements. So the moral of the story – do these tests!

Remember to read the instructions before you start and record your results in the table on page 111.

Instructions

- Do not take these tests if your doctor has told you not to exercise, or if you have chest pain, joint pain, dizziness or uncontrolled high blood pressure.
- You can do them with a partner or alone. Test two is best done with the help of a partner.
- Try to do your best on each test but do not overexert yourself.
- Before starting, warm up with five to eight minutes of walking, rolling your shoulders and swinging your arms.

Test 1: 30-second Chair Stand

This test measures your lower body strength.

1. Sit in a chair, the seat height ideally 43cm (17 inches), with feet flat on the floor and your arms crossed over your chest.
2. Count the number of times in 30 seconds you can come to a full stand.

Test 2: Two-minute Knee Lift

This test measures the endurance of your heart and legs.

1. Let your partner find the point midway between your hip and knee.
2. Mark that target height on a table leg or a wall.
3. March on the spot for two minutes and count how often the right leg reaches the target height.

Test 3a: Sit and Reach (for the over-60s)

This test measures the flexibility of your lower spine and hamstrings, the muscles at the back of the leg. (If you are under 60, please skip this test and perform test 3b instead.)

1. Place a chair against a wall so it is secure and won't move. Sit on the edge. Place one foot flat on the floor and extend the other leg out straight so the heel is on the floor.
2. With arms outstretched, reach to the toe on the extended leg and make a note of the position of your fingertips.
3. Record the centimetres or inches short of your toes with a (–), or put a (+) in front of your score for the measurement past your toes.

Test 3b: Sit and Reach (for the under-60s)

You will need to remove your shoes for this test. Sit on the floor with your legs straight out in front of you. Your feet should be facing the ceiling. Lean forward slowly as far as possible and hold the stretch for two seconds. Make sure there are no jerky movements, and that the fingertips remain level and the legs flat. The score is the distance before (negative) or beyond (positive) the toes. Repeat the test twice and record the best score.

How Did You Do?

The following scores show the average range for people in various age groups. If you scored below the range in any of the tests, this is a good indicator that you need to pay more attention to this aspect of fitness. Remember, however, that putting in extra effort to gain faster improvement can be false economy.

Start off slowly and have faith in my plan, which has been developed to help you progress your fitness slowly.

M= Male, F = Female

Number of stands (Test 1):

Age	45–49	50–54	55–59	60–64	65–69	70–74	75–79	80–84	85–89
F	15–22	14–19	13–18	12–17	11–16	10–15	10–15	9–14	8–13
M	12–23	14–21	16–20	14–19	12–18	12–17	11–17	10–15	8–14

Number of steps (Test 2):

Age	45–49	50–54	55–59	60–64	65–69	70–74	75–79	80–84	85–89
F	82–120	78–118	77–112	75–107	73–107	68–101	68–100	60–91	55–85
M	88–131	86–125	84–120	82–115	80–110	73–109	71–103	59–91	52–86

Reach (Test 3a) (measured in inches):

AGE	60–64	65–69	70–74	75–79	80–84	85–89
F	-0.5–+5.0	-0.5–+4.5	-1.0–+4.0	-1.5–+3.5	-2.0–+3.0	-2.5–+2.5
M	-2.5–+4.0	-3.0–+3.0	-3.5–+2.5	-4.0–+2.0	-5.5–+1.5	-5.5–+0.5

Reach (Test 3b) (measured in centimetres):

	Men	Women
super	> +27	> +30
excellent	+17 to +27	+21 to +30
good	+6 to +16	+11 to +20
average	0 to +5	+1 to +10
fair	–8 to –1	–7 to 0
poor	–19 to –9	–14 to –8
very poor	< –20	< –15

Your Test Results

Use this table to record your scores before and after the six-week plan.

TEST	Your Start Score (start of 6-week plan)	Your End Score (end of 6-week plan)
30-sec Chair Stand measures strength	0	
2-min Knee Lift measures endurance	0	
Sit and Reach measures flexibility	— 15 cm	

Remember, it really doesn't matter how you score at the beginning of your six-week plan. The most important thing is to establish a bench mark against which you can measure your improvement. Your first score will be dependent partly upon the activity you are currently doing and partly on your genetics. For example, your flexibility score for the Sit and Reach test will not depend only on the sort of mobility movements you are familiar with; it will also be influenced by the shape of your joints, and ligament and tendon length, all of which are partly genetically determined.

Armed with the knowledge of where you and your body are now, you are ready to start the GI Walking Diet.

6 The Six-week Exercise Plan

Do it for yourself or do it for others you care about. But just do it!

Your six-week exercise plan has three components:
1. The walking plan
2. The strength plan
3. The flexibility plan

The three plans work together to:
- Improve your posture
- Increase your energy levels
- Help you lose weight
- Make you look and feel much better – and younger – in six weeks

I have devised the exercise plan in line with current scientific research, so you can feel confident that your efforts will be rewarded. Each plan has a series of simple and easy-to-follow exercises, with clear descriptions and pictures, as well as lots of ways to tailor each exercise to your ability, guiding you to an achievable result.

In this chapter you'll also find a special balance plan (page 154) and a section on posture (page 167). Although optional, the balance plan will be particularly beneficial if you suffer from osteoporosis, are concerned about arthritis, are recovering from an operation, or are serious about reducing your risk of falling. Like all the plans I'll guide you through, it is straightforward, clearly illustrated and won't take ages to complete.

If you are embarking on an exercise journey for the first time, you may think there's a lot to do, but the great news is you don't do everything every day. The six-week daily plan on pages 161–6 is clearly laid out, guiding you to get fitter, trimmer and more energetic. If you are already fairly active, you'll find tips to help you progress your exercise routine, to enhance your body shape and deliver results that may have previously eluded you.

Finding an Exercise Professional

If you would like to work with an exercise professional, be careful: the exercise industry has not been that well-regulated in the past. Ask questions – good instructors not only know their stuff but are also sensitive, caring and empathic. Develop a relationship with a good one and they are worth their weight in gold.

Make sure you find an exercise professional who:

◆ Can teach you which exercises to do and how intensively to do them
◆ Has a degree, usually in Exercise Sciences, but perhaps in another health field
◆ Is certified by a credible organization (such as ACSM, APTA) and may have special training to work with older adults

Start the programme slowly. When in doubt, ask questions, flip through this book or log on to my website www.joannahall.com and look at the Question and Answer section.

How Hard Should I Be Exercising?

When starting to exercise, don't begin too intensively. Studies show that people who exercise too hard initially tend to drop out of exercise and don't maintain their fitness.

Use the following table to gauge how hard you are actually working. In structured exercise sessions – when you put on your trainers and exercise kit and set aside specific time to complete your plan – you should be working at a 'perceived exertion rate' of between 5 and 8. When you are doing accumulated exercise – the physical activity you build up during the day – you should be working at a perceived exertion rate of between 3 and 6. As you get fitter, you will find that the exercises you started with become easier. To keep your body responding to exercise, burning calories and reducing your body fat, you will need to keep pushing yourself so your body receives a workout at a rate of between 5 and 8.

Perceived Exertion Rate

Rating	Perceived Exertion	Examples of Exertion
0	Nothing at all	Lying completely still in bed, sleeping.
1	Very weak	Watching TV or film in the cinema, sitting in a meeting, sewing or reading a book.
2	Weak	Browsing shops, playing the piano, typing, filling the washing machine.
3	Moderate	Walking the dog, walking to work, playing leisurely game of doubles tennis.
4	Somewhat strong	Climbing an escalator, carrying shopping up several flights of stairs, cycling.
5	Strong, somewhat hard	Manually mowing the lawn, walking very briskly.
6	Fairly strong, hard	Walking briskly up a hill, pushing a pram up a slope, digging in the garden.
7	Strong; can do for only a limited time.	Fast jogging or running, carrying furniture or lifting weights in a gym.
8	Very strong.	Running fast to catch the last bus home, skipping with a rope, circuit training.
9	Very, very hard	Running in a competitive race.
10	Maximum effort	Running for your life.

Clothing/Sweat Factor	Chat Factor
Warm clothes or covers required as body not generating heat.	Can chat to your heart's content – if awake!
Clothes dependent on temperature of environment. No sweat.	Can chat to your heart's content.
Clothes dependent on temperature of environment. No sweat.	Can chat to your heart's content.
Feel a little warm in the clothes you are wearing. Starting to sweat.	Able to talk comfortably.
You need to remove an item of clothing. Starting to perspire.	Able to talk but not sing.
Need to take off a layer of clothes to avoid sweating.	Able to hold a breathy conversation.
Perspiration felt on body and face.	Able to hold a conversation but feels a little uncomfortable.
Definite sweating on face and body.	Able to hold a sporadic conversation with short pauses.
Body feeling very warm. Sweating. Light clothing worn.	Unable to hold a continuous conversation.
Body feels very hot. Sweating during and after activity.	Unable to hold a conversation.
Whole body and head feel very hot.	Unable to speak.

Warming Up and Cooling Down

It is important to warm up before any exercise session to get your mind and body ready for your workout. Don't skip the warm-up thinking it will save you time – this is false economy and may lead to injury. In as little as three to five minutes you can mobilize your major joints with shoulder rolls, some side bends and full body stretches. Add a few squats and knee lifts to your chest. Brisk marching on the spot and running up and down stairs will increase your body temperature.

Don't forget to cool down after each workout. For ease, you can repeat your warm-up in reverse, decreasing the size of your movements and finishing with the stretches to lengthen and stretch your body.

Warm-up Stretches

Standing Hamstring Stretch

Stand with good posture. Extend one leg out in front of you. Bend the back knee and flex forward from the hips. Make sure you contract your abdominals as you extend forward. Lift up out of the hips and check they are level. To help you, imagine you need to balance a glass of water on each side of your lower back.

> **Joanna's Top Tip:** To progress the stretch, lift your leg and rest it on a bench or low step or chair.

Standing Quad Stretch

Stand with good posture, using a chair to help with balance. Lift one leg, bending at the knee, holding the laces of your shoe in your hand. Keep the knees together. Gently press your hips forward as you extend up through your spine.

> **Joanna's Top Tip:** If you have limited flexibility, rest your foot on a chair and press your hips forward.

Lying Gluteal Stretch

Lie on your back. Extend one leg down to the floor and draw the other knee into the chest, holding the knee behind the knee cap. Make sure you contract your abdominals so that you stretch the gluteals effectively.

Joanna's Top Tip: Focus on stretching the straight leg away from your body and you will feel a stretch over your front hip.

Lying Spine Twist

Lie on your back with your legs extended flat on the floor. Lift one knee towards the chest and gently ease it across the opposite side of your body, supporting it with the opposite hand. As far as possible, keep the knee at 90 degrees to the torso. You are aiming to get the inside of the knee to the other side of the floor. Breathe in a controlled manner and do only what is comfortable for you. To change sides, contract your abdominals and release the leg to the floor, then repeat with the other leg.

Joanna's Top Tip: To increase the stretch, place your foot on the opposing knee and press down gently.

Inner Thigh Stretch

Sit with good posture. Place the soles of your feet together and allow the knees to drop open.

Joanna's Top Tip: To progress this position, gently apply a little pressure on your inner thighs with your elbows and forearms. Your hands should be resting lightly on your ankles.

Lying Full Body Stretch

Lie on your back, extending your arms above your head. Gently stretch and lengthen through the whole body from your fingertips to your toes. Your lower back may lift slightly away from the floor. Breathe gently and hold for up to 30 seconds. Slowly bring your arms down by your sides.

> **Joanna's Top Tip:** Allow your lower spine to come off the floor and really focus on extending your body.

Standing Tricep Stretch

Standing with good posture, lift one arm above the head and drop the palm of the hand behind the head between the shoulder blades. Lift the other arm and support the stretching arm either by pressing gently from the front on the soft fleshy part of the arm or above on the elbow. This stretch can also be performed sitting down.

> **Joanna's Top Tip:** If you have limited movement in your shoulders, holding a towel behind your back can help ease the shoulder joint.

All Fours Trapezius Stretch

On all fours, with your wrists under the shoulders and knees under the hips, slide one hand, palm upwards, between your knee and arm and away from the body. Gently allow the shoulder of the extended arm to relax and open. You should feel a gentle opening behind the shoulders.

> **Joanna's Top Tip:** Keep the elbow off the floor but focus on allowing the shoulder blade to open and 'dip' down to the floor.

The Walking Plan

When beginning a walking programme, it's important not to set unrealistic goals. This can lead to disappointment and put a stop to all your healthy behaviour and good intentions.

> My walking plan is all about you feeling supported in your fitness and health efforts, being in control and able to complete it with confidence and a sense of fulfilment.

Not everyone will start at the same level. To help you follow an appropriate programme for you, I have designed two walking plans:

1. **The entry level** is suitable for those new to walking or suffering from a condition that may limit their rate of progression.
2. **The advanced level** is suitable for those already following a walking programme or used to being physically active, who enjoy a faster rate of progress.

Each week you will be asked to do a little more, apart from in week four, when I ask you to repeat week three. This allows your body to rest, recuperate and benefit from all your efforts. Do follow your respective walking plan: it is specifically designed to be effective, and even if you are super-keen and feel like racing ahead, your extra efforts will not necessarily get you closer to your goal. So have confidence in the programme and what I am asking you to do, and you will achieve fantastic results.

Entry Level Walking Plan

The entry level walking plan has been designed so that you progress at a steady rate but still get fitter and feel better. Completed in conjunction with your six-week eating plan, it will help you lose excess weight. However, your weight loss may be more gradual than on the advanced level walking plan, as your total energy expenditure will be less.

Entry Level Countdown

Step 1: Establish Baseline Number of Steps per Day

To do this, wear your pedometer for seven days and keep track of your steps per day over a typical week. You can record your daily total in the chart below:

Day	Number of steps walked
1	
2	
3	
4	
5	
6	
7	

The greatest number of steps I walked in any one day in the past seven days was _____. This is my starting baseline.

Step 2: Complete Fitness Walking Test

This is a timed walk performed at the start, middle and end of your six-week plan. Your progress is monitored by recording your heart rate, and the length of time it takes you to complete the distance. For the entry level, test yourself over a quarter of a kilometre. (Advanced level walkers should test themselves over half a kilometre.)

As you get fitter over the six weeks, your heart muscle becomes stronger and is able to pump more efficiently the oxygenated blood your body requires. This means your walking time should be faster and your heart rate lower.

Date: .... Start of six-week plan		Date: .... During week four		Date: .... End of six-week plan	
Time to complete:	......	Time to complete:	......	Time to complete:	......
Start heart rate:	......	Start heart rate:	......	Start heart rate:	......
Finish heart rate:	......	Finish heart rate:	......	Finish heart rate:	......
Post–1 minute recovery HR:	......	Post–1 minute recovery HR:	......	Post–1 minute recovery HR:	......

- **Start heart rate:** This is your resting heart rate (HR) taken immediately before you start your timed walk. Find your pulse either at the wrist or neck (carotid) and record your HR for 10 seconds and multiply by six. Record it in the box above.

- **Finish heart rate:** This is your heart rate taken immediately after completing the timed walk. Find your pulse and record your heart rate for a full 60 seconds. Since your heart rate will start to slow down over the minute, it is important to count your HR for the full 60 seconds to get an accurate measure of how your body is responding.
- **Post-1 minute recovery heart rate:** After you have recorded your finish HR, wait one minute and then record your HR for a further 60 seconds. This will give you the greatest indication of how your fitness has improved. Your recovery heart rate is indicative of how quickly your HR comes back to its normal resting level. The faster it returns to its normal level, the more efficient your heart is, and the more able it is to cope with changes in the workloads you place upon it.

Find yourself a route that is flat, safe and even. You could do the test in a park or even along a well-lit stretch of path, using it as a 'there and back' route. Don't panic if you don't have an exact distance to test yourself over, but do repeat your test over the same route each time so you can compare your results.

Week One

Aim each day to make the number of steps you walk equal to or above the highest number you achieved during the baseline test (see page 125).

For example, if your highest daily step value over the seven days of the test was 3,590, you need to complete at least 3,590 steps each day in week one. Walking more is a bonus but you must aim to walk at least this amount for seven consecutive days.

Week Two

Aim to add 1,000 steps to your baseline on five out of seven days plus 3 minutes' continuous intensity walking on three out of seven days.

Week Three

Aim to add an extra 2,000 steps to your baseline on five out of seven days.

Week Four

Repeat week three. Complete the walking fitness test again, and record your results.

Week Five

Aim to add 3,000 steps to your baseline on five out of seven days, plus 4 minutes' continuous intensity walking on three out of seven days.

Week Six

Add an extra 5,000 steps to your baseline on five out of seven days, plus 5 minutes' continuous intensity walking on three out of seven days. Complete the walking fitness test again and record your results.

Advanced Level Walking Plan

Your rate of progression on this plan is a little more challenging than on the entry level plan.

Advanced Level Countdown

Step 1: Establish Baseline Number of Steps per Day

To do this, keep track of your steps per day over a typical three-day period.

Day	Number of steps walked
1	
2	
3	

The greatest number of steps I walked in any one day in the past three days: _____. My baseline average (total number of steps over three days divided by three): _____

Step 2: Complete Fitness Walking Test

To do this, see page 126.

Week One

Aim to add 2,000 steps to your baseline average on five out of seven days.

Week Two

Aim to add 2,000 steps to your baseline on five out of seven days, plus 6 minutes' continuous intensity walking on three out of seven days.

Week Three

Aim to add an extra 4,000 steps to your baseline on five out of seven days.

Week Four

Repeat week three. Complete the walking fitness test again, and record your results.

Week Five

Aim to add 6,000 steps to your baseline on five out of seven days, plus 8 minutes' continuous intensity walking on three out of seven days.

Week Six

Add an extra 6,000 steps to your baseline on five out of seven days, plus 10 minutes' continuous intensity walking on three out of seven days. Complete the walking fitness test again, and record your results.

At a Glance Guide to Walking

Before you start your walking plan, you may find it helpful to ask yourself the following questions. It will help you put together an approach that best suits you.

Where Will I Walk?

Before you start, it's a good idea to plan your walking route. Perhaps the local park appeals, or maybe you'd prefer a route around the block or along a country lane. Wherever you decide to walk, make sure your route is well-lit if you will be walking after dark. A pavement can be a good, level surface but grass or a footpath may be less jarring on your joints. Be aware of how even the surface is. If you always walk the same way on a road, I'd advise you to change the direction of your route every other trip. This is because the camber of the road can be curved, causing your ankles to rotate and leading to uneven foot strikes and potential injury.

Consider exercising with a partner or friend, or in a supervised facility. This can be very sociable, keep you motivated and may help your confidence if you know you have someone on hand to help you.

Can I Do Other Types of Exercise Too?

Although walking is the simplest and most accessible form of endurance exercise and the basis of your six-week plan, you can complement it with other activities such as cycling, swimming, rowing and stair-stepping. All are great!

What Will I Need?

Get well-made equipment, such as walking shoes with good stability (see page 68). You will probably also need a good waterproof top and a hat to protect you from the elements. A good pedometer will also prove invaluable (see page 60).

How Hard Should I Exercise?

+ Monitor your exercise intensity (see page 161) and duration, and record the time on the charts provided. Use the Perceived Exertion Rate for an easy way to monitor how hard you are working (see page 116).
+ Start each session slowly and give yourself at least 5 minutes to warm up (see page 118).
+ Judge how your body feels. Being aware of your body before, during and after you exercise will help improve your physical awareness.
+ Remember, you should never be in pain or unable to speak when you exercise.
+ If you are on any medication that affects your heart rate, talk to your doctor about what you are planning to do.
+ Always start slowly but plan to work your body a little harder as weeks go by. The six-week plan will automatically provide you with a safe, effective and progressive programme.

How Long Should My Walking Sessions Be?

+ At first, your walks may last 5 minutes, but plan to increase the duration gradually. My six-week walking plan organizes your progression for you.
+ If you prefer, you can break your exercise up into bouts of 6 minutes.
+ For best results, try to complete the prescribed timings for continuous exercise each day.
+ Exercising for 30–45 minutes is ideal, and the end goal of your six-week plan. Don't panic if this sounds too much – it can be made up of endurance work for your heart as well as strength and flexibility exercises.

How Often Should I Exercise?

◆ The walking plan needs to be completed on at least five days each week.

◆ Try to have non-consecutive rest days. You can still do your mobility or strength exercises on the non-walking days. If you are super-keen and do endurance exercise daily, try to alternate the days on which you do weight-bearing exercises (such as walking) with those when you do non-weight-bearing ones (such as cycling or swimming).

The Strength Plan

Exercise can usually be done with little risk or expense. The biggest risk is not starting!

Strength and Ageing

Strength generally deteriorates as we age, partly due to a loss of lean body mass or muscle. Our body's ability to send the correct message from the brain to the targeted muscle – a process called 'recruitment' – also declines with age. Studies have shown that muscle recruitment is at its optimum when we are 25, then slowly declines to about 40 per cent by the time we are 80. Over the age of 50, the decline in muscle mass is accompanied by this decline in recruitment. The following strength plan will not only enhance the development of muscle mass essential for raising your metabolic rate and strong bones, but will also stimulate the correct recruitment of your nerve fibres. So your muscles will be able to get stronger faster.

The Benefits of Strength Training

Older males and females can experience significant gains in strength and muscle mass after participating in a resistance training programme. This may be due to an increase in muscle recruitment and improvements in lean muscle mass. Even if you have an injury or restricted joint movement and are unable to train all limbs, don't be put off. Studies have shown that in older adults there is a possibility of a 'cross-education' of responses between the trained and untrained part of the body. In both older males and females, resistance training involving the use of one limb created significant improvements in the strength of the untrained limb.

Who Should Do It?

Fifty plus is an excellent time to start or resume a strength training programme. After the age of 45 there is a critical period when muscle mass is reduced. This leads to a decrease in resting metabolic rate and calorie burning. Resistance training at this time – specifically the strength plan – can have a significant effect.

How Long Does it Take?

When you start the plan, you will be doing fewer repetitions of each exercise, so the programme may take you around 8 minutes. At the end of the six weeks, with the extra exercise and the additional repetitions, it should take you closer to 12 minutes. This plan can easily be integrated into your walking programme, either in the middle or when you have returned from your walking session.

Alternatively, you may prefer to set aside specific time to do it. If so, make sure you are thoroughly warmed up and complete a few stretches afterwards. You'll find tips on warming up and cooling down on page 118.

The Exercises

The following exercises are designed to improve your strength. For balance, you may find it helpful to use a chair, wall or park bench. For instructions on how often to perform the exercises during the plan, see page 141.

Forward Lunge

1. Start in a standing position with feet shoulder-width apart.
2. Take a large step forward with the right leg, keeping the upper body straight.
3. Bend the back knee until it almost touches the floor. Your front knee should be aligned with your front foot. If you drew an imaginary line through the middle of your knee cap, it should line up with your second toe.

4. During the lunge, the upper body should remain straight and in an upright position, not bending forward or backward.

5. Return to the upright position and repeat the lunge 8–15 times.

6. Return to the initial position and repeat the forward lunge with the other leg. Repeat 8–15 times.

Squat

1. Start in a standing position with legs wide.

2. Your feet and knees should be angled slightly outwards, with the knees pointing in the same direction as the feet.

3. Keeping your back straight, lean forward slightly at the hip (not bending at the waist or upper back).

4. To perform the squat, bend your legs at the knees, keeping the back straight until you reach a 90-degree angle.

5. Rise quickly back to the starting position.

6. Repeat the squat 8–15 times.

Never bend at the waist or upper back during the squat. Always keep your back straight.

Sideways Lunge

1. Start in a standing position with feet shoulder-width apart.
2. Take a big step to the side with your right foot, with the right knee and foot pointing out at a 45-degree angle. Your weight shifts to the right as the foot lunges right.
3. Use the right leg as a spring to bring the right leg back to the starting point.
4. Do not turn or twist the upper body. The knee should track in line with the foot during the lunge.
5. After 8–15 repetitions with the right leg, repeat 8–15 times with the left leg.

Chair Raise

You will need an armless chair for this exercise.

1. Stand with your back to the chair with your feet hip-distance apart. Feet and knees should be angled slightly outwards, with the knees pointing in the same direction as the feet.

2. Keep the back straight and lean forward slightly, bending at the hip (not at the waist or upper back).

3. Lower your thighs towards the chair until you are almost, but not quite, sitting down.

4. Rise quickly, coming back to the starting position.

5. Repeat the chair raise 8–15 times.

Never bend at the waist or upper back during the chair raise. Always keep the back straight.

Heel/Toe Raise

Heel Raise

1. Start in a standing position with feet shoulder-width apart.
2. Lift both heels off the floor, standing on the toes and balls of the feet. Extend your arms upwards.
3. Hold this position for 3–4 seconds.
4. Lower your heels to the floor slowly and rock back on to the heels, lifting the toes off the floor. Extend your arms forward.

Toe Raise

5. Hold this position for 3–4 seconds.
6. Lower the toes to the floor slowly, returning to the starting position.
7. Repeat the heel/toe raise 8–15 times.

Alternating Lunges (introduced in week two)

1. Perform a sequence of forward, sideways and backward lunges, always returning to the centre after each lunge.
2. With the backward lunge, take a step backward and perform the lunge the same way as the forward lunge – bend the back knee until it almost touches the floor.
3. Perform the sequence for 8–15 repetitions with the right leg leading, and then with the left leg leading.

If All These Seem Too Easy ...

The progressions outlined in the plan below will challenge you over the weeks. However, if you are already involved in a strength programme you may find these exercises too easy. To make them more challenging, add a small set of hand weights, holding one in each hand with your arms crossed across your chest. Holding your arms in this position will initially challenge your balance as you perform these exercises, so do try it without weights first. Add weights up to 10kg, starting with 2kg. Remember, the most important thing is your technique

— ensure you master this correctly before adding more weight. If you are serious about your training, you may wish to invest in a weighted vest, which can load weight on to your torso without any undue strain on your limbs. However, no additional weights were used in my research for this plan, and benefits were still experienced in strength, performance and bone density. So the good news is you don't have to push yourself that hard to get great results.

Progression of Exercises: Sets, Repetitions and Weight

Repetitions or 'reps' are the number of times an exercise is repeated. Sets are the number of times you do an exercise with its given number of reps.

Exercises	Sets	Repetitions
Week 1		
Forward Lunge	1	8
Squat	1	8
Sideways Lunge	1	8
Chair Raise	1	8
Heel/Toe Raise	1	8
Week 2		
Forward Lunge	1	12
Squat	1	12
Sideways Lunge	1	12
Chair Raise	1	12
Heel/Toe Raise	1	12
Alternating Lunges	1	6

Exercises	Sets	Repetitions
Week 3		
Forward Lunge	1	12
Squat	1	12
Sideways Lunge	1	12
Chair Raise	1	12
Heel/Toe Raise	1	12
Alternating Lunges	1	10
Week 4		
Forward Lunge	2	8
Squat	2	8
Sideways Lunge	2	8
Chair Raise	1	12
Heel/Toe Raise	1	12
Alternating Lunges	1	10
Week 5		
Forward Lunge	2	12
Squat	2	12
Sideways Lunge	2	12
Chair Raise	1	12
Heel/Toe Raise	1	12
Alternating Lunges	1	12

Exercises	Sets	Repetitions
Week 6		
Forward Lunge	2	12
Squat	2	12
Sideways Lunge	2	12
Chair Raise	1	15
Heel/Toe Raise	1	12
Alternating Lunges	1	12

Other Exercise Ideas

Strength can be increased with activities that build muscle and bone such as callisthenics, Pilates, weightlifting or rowing. If you are already enjoying these then you can complement your programme, but do remember to have a rest day.

At a Glance Guide to Strength Training

Before you start your strength plan, ask yourself the following questions:

Where Should I Exercise?

- Consider joining a health club or gym – or work with a fully qualified personal trainer – to help guide you through the six-week plan. However, you can do the exercises at home if you prefer.
- As you become familiar with the strength exercises, you can perform them as part of your walking plan, either while out and about on your walk or when you return home.

How Often and for How Long Should I Exercise?

- You only need to complete your strength plan two or three times each week, and it can take as little as 10 minutes. Even at the end of week six, your whole strength workout should take no longer than 15 minutes.
- Rest days are important to give your muscles a chance to recuperate. Think of your muscles as loaves of bread that need time to prove. Ideally, leave at least one rest day between your strength sessions.

What Do I Need?

- You don't need to use weights – all you need is your own body weight.
- Follow the exercise pictures and descriptions in this book. They are specifically designed for you.
- If exercising at a health club or gym, seek advice from a qualified fitness instructor, personal trainer, physio or physical therapist.
- Learn the strength and flexibility exercises so you can perform them whether at home, travelling or in the gym.

How Hard Should I Exercise?

- Each of the strength exercises progresses gradually over the six weeks. This is necessary to help your body get fitter and adapt effectively to the exercises you are asking it to perform. It means you will not only see great results but will also be exercising in a safe and enjoyable way.

- The strength exercises progress by introducing a few more repetitions or adjusting your position to make it a little harder each week.

How Should I Perform the Exercises?

- Make sure you breathe smoothly throughout the exercises. It's normal practice to breathe once for each repetition.

- Always complete each part of the strength exercise with control. Remember, you are in control of your body. Don't let the exercise control you!

What if I Ache Afterwards?

You may be a little sore during the first week, but it will pass. This is perfectly normal as your body adjusts to new stimuli. If, however, the pain persists for more than three days, it's likely you were a little overenthusiastic. Next time, ease back a little, and always complement your strength exercises with the flexibility plan (page 146).

What Results Can I Expect to See?

- Regardless of your age, you will become much stronger – probably 25–100 per cent stronger in each muscle. This has a huge impact on what you can do.

- Research shows the biggest improvements take place during the first six weeks! So what are you waiting for?

The Flexibility Plan

Flexibility, Mobility and Ageing

As we get older, the range of mobility around each joint is reduced as the connective tissue becomes less pliable. This can cause a gradual loss of flexibility and coordination, and can directly affect balance. To preserve or restore the range of motion and flexibility around each joint, you don't need to spend hours stretching. A small selection of simple exercises can make you feel better and your body more agile. In fact, improving your mobility and balance is the foundation of your exercise success.

You'll see real benefits by doing these exercises three times a week, but you can do them every day if you find you enjoy them.

The Exercises

Chest Opening

1. Stand facing a wall, about a foot length away.
2. Lift one arm out to the side at shoulder height, so the palm of the hand is flat on the wall and the elbow and shoulder are close to it.
3. Slowly start to turn your feet away from your outstretched arm. Try to turn them through 90 degrees so your torso is now sideways to the wall and your arm is still in contact with it. You should start to feel a nice opening across the front of the chest.
4. If comfortable, try to rotate the feet a little further away from the direction of the outstretched arm. Hold for 10–30 seconds then repeat on the other side.

Lying Side Rotation

1. Lying flat on your back with legs extended, gently bring one leg in at a time so your knees are lifted off the floor and over your hips.
2. Take the arms out to the side, level with the shoulders, to provide some balance.
3. Keeping your tummy muscles contracted and both your knees together, slowly lower your knees to the left.
4. Try to keep the knees close to your waist, rather than stretched out away from the body. You should feel a gentle stretch on your spine, and across your outer thigh and waist. Exactly where you feel the stretch will depend where you are most tight.
5. Hold for 10–30 seconds, pull your tummy muscles in and repeat on the other side.

Wall Rolls

1. Stand with your back to a wall. Adjust your feet to be a little way from the wall so each part of your back, hips, lower spine, waist, torso and head are all touching the wall.
2. With the knees slightly bent, slowly drop your head forward, chin to chest, as you peel each part of your spine, from your head to your hips, slowly away from the wall. Try to create as tight a curl as possible through your spine, challenging each vertebra to progressively come off the wall. Let your arms hang loosely by your side as you roll down.
3. Keep the hips in contact with the wall throughout, and slowly uncurl to an upright position, placing each vertebra back in contact with the wall.
4. Try not to rush this exercise. One whole roll-down cycle should take at least four counts down and four counts up. Aim to do 4–8 of these.

Sticking Points

In this exercise you are likely to experience 'sticking points'. This is when you find it difficult to peel your spine off the wall bit by bit, and instead your spine seems to come away in sections. Your personal sticking points will depend on the mobility of your spine and any particular muscular imbalances. Do persist with this exercise. At first it may seem difficult, but as you continue and complete your other mobility exercises as well, you will see big improvements in the movement of your spine.

Cat Curls

1. Form a box position on your hands and knees, hips over knees and shoulders over wrists. Your limbs should form straight sides of a square box, and your back should be flat.

2. Pull your tummy muscles in firmly, arching your spine up towards the ceiling. Hold this position, breathing smoothly, feeling your belly being scooped up to your spine.

3. Now reverse this position, passing through the flat back position you started with, gently arching your spine in the opposite direction so it dips down to the floor. Ensure your tummy and pelvic floor muscles are still being pulled in to support your spine.

4. Aim to do 4–8 complete arches.

Challenge Your Balance

To make this exercise harder, you can challenge your balance. In the flat back position, slowly lift one leg off the floor, extending it back into a straight line behind you. Pull tightly up through your abdominals, pelvic floor and bottom to provide internal stability. Lower the leg and repeat on the other side. Once this feels relatively easy, you can challenge yourself further by performing the leg lifts with your eyes shut. This tests your sensory receptors responsible for good balance.

Upward Dog Presses

1. Start in the all-fours position, as in Cat Curls (above), with your toes tucked beneath you.
2. Adjust your weight so you are supporting yourself on your hands and toes, and slowly lift the hips to the ceiling.
3. Press your heels back to the floor so you feel a stretch on the back of your calves and hamstrings.
4. Try to press the chest away from your hands and backward towards your hips, as this will help you form a 'V' position with your body.

Work Up to it

This exercise is quite challenging. It may feel more like a strength exercise at first since you are supporting your weight in your arms and legs. You don't have to do the full position straightaway. You can progress gradually by performing small lifts, taking your knees off the floor and supporting your weight on your hands and feet. Rise in and out of this position 4–5 times, pulling up through your abdominals, pelvic floor and bottom.

Better flexibility can also be achieved through activities such as yoga, Pilates, ballet and martial arts.

At a Glance Guide to Flexibility Training

- The flexibility exercises are probably the easiest ones to start. You don't need any equipment – you can even do them in your night clothes, or any other comfortable clothing, so there's no excuse not to do them first thing in the morning.
- Even though the flexibility exercises may feel gentler than the other components of the exercise plan, it's still important to start slowly.
- Don't strain your muscles with overenthusiastic stretching. Respect your body and it'll do you far more favours.
- Any time of day is good – but doing the exercises in the morning may get the day off to a good start.
- Modify the position depending on your ability. For example, you can do some of the exercises seated or on the floor.
- Breathe smoothly and evenly throughout. Try not to hold your breath when concentrating.

The Balance Plan (Optional)

Balance and Ageing

Our balance deteriorates from around the age of 40. Tiny sensory hairs in the inner ear lose their sensitivity, decreasing our ability to detect balance changes. As we have seen, balance is also affected by the gradual loss of flexibility and coordination associated with ageing.

The Benefits of Balance Training

Balance is important for good posture, helping you look trimmer and use your muscles in the right way. Good balance reduces the risk of conditions such as repetitive strain injury and niggling wear-and-tear injuries such as a troublesome back, aching knees or stiff shoulders. Most of all, balance is crucial for reducing the risks of falls. This may sound dramatic, but when you trip on a pavement, having good balance can make the difference between you falling to the ground on your knees or being able to stay upright. Mobility works in conjunction with balance, as a restricted range of motion in joints affects how you can recruit your muscles and centre your body.

Who Should Do it?

Everyone can benefit from this plan but it's particularly useful for those in their late 30s and beyond. Good balance will enhance your ability to move and be physically active, which means your body will keep burning calories efficiently, maintaining your weight and health for longer.

How Long Does it Take?

Only 7 minutes – now that really is a small section of your day.

> Balance can also be helped by yoga and martial arts, especially t'ai chi. Posture exercises and weight machines can help by strengthening the legs and lower back muscles.

The Exercises

To improve your balance and mobility, perform the following exercises three times a week. All you need is a chair and a Dyna Band or pair of old tights, so you can do them at home or when away.

Leg Back Lifts

1. Stand with good posture, holding on to a chair.
2. Take 3 seconds to lift one leg behind you slowly, squeezing your calf close to your thigh.
3. Hold for a second then slowly lower for 3 seconds.
4. Repeat with the other leg.

Leg Front Lifts

1. Stand sideways next to a chair or wall. Do not lean against the chair or wall – just use it for support if necessary, holding on with your hand.
2. Slowly raise your right knee for 3 seconds, bringing it as close to your chest as possible.
3. Hold for 1 second and then take 3 seconds to lower it slowly.
4. Repeat with the other leg.

Make sure you stretch up through your back as you do this so the knee comes to the chest, and not the chest to the knee.

Side Lifts

1. Stand sideways next to a chair or wall. Do not lean against the chair or wall – just use it for support if necessary, holding on with your hand. Lift your leg out to the side, taking 3 seconds to lift it as far as it will comfortably go. Make sure you keep your back straight as you lift.
2. Hold for 1 second and then slowly lower your leg, taking 3 seconds.
3. Repeat on the other leg.

As you lift, focus on contracting your pelvic floor muscles to help your balance. The pelvic floor muscles are the ones you squeeze to stop the flow of urine.

Achilles Ankle Strengthener

When running or walking, the foot naturally tends to roll in or 'pronate' with each foot strike. In some people, over-pronation can cause consequent pain in the Achilles tendon. This exercise will help strengthen the Achilles tendon and encourage blood circulation to that part of the body. It is a particularly useful exercise to include as part of your warm-up if you have experienced Achilles problems before.

1. Stand with good posture, weight even on both feet.
2. Slowly draw your weight to the left leg, lifting your right leg off the floor.
3. Close your eyes and try to balance for 30 seconds. This is challenging so do build up to it.
4. Repeat on the other side. The higher you lift the supporting leg, the more challenging for your Achilles tendon.

The Wobbly Knee Beater

Weak knees and pain around or beneath the kneecap is often due to an imbalance between the muscles on the inside and outside of the joint. This exercise targets the weaker medialis muscles of the quadriceps, which attach around the inside of the knee, helping to strengthen these important postural muscles. This is a good exercise for anyone with weak knees who is embarking on a walking or running programme.

1. Tie a Dyna Band or pair of old tights securely around your right knee and attach it to something stable, such as a table leg.
2. Stand with your left foot behind you, heel slightly raised.
3. Slowly bend your right knee, making sure it is correctly aligned over your foot.
4. Straighten your leg and repeat 6–8 times, then change to your left leg.

If All These Seem Too Easy ...

To make these exercises more challenging, perform them with less support from your hands – try them with just one finger holding on to the chair or wall. To challenge yourself further, try doing the exercises with your eyes closed. This is much harder than you might imagine, as your eyes provide an essential reference point for your brain to balance the body.

Six-week Exercise Plan – Week 1

	Mon	Tue	Wed	Thu	Fri	Sat	Sun
Walking Step target: Steps done: Exertion rate:							
Strength* Minutes: Notes:							
Flexibility† Minutes: Notes:							
Balance* (Optional) Minutes: Notes:							

*Preferably three non-consecutive days
†Aim for at least three sessions per week

Six-week Exercise Plan – Week 2

	Mon	Tue	Wed	Thu	Fri	Sat	Sun
Walking Step target: Steps done: Exertion rate:							
Strength* Minutes: Notes:							
Flexibility† Minutes: Notes:							
Balance* (Optional) Minutes: Notes:							

*Preferably three non-consecutive days
†Aim for at least three sessions per week

Six-week Exercise Plan – Week 3

	Mon	Tue	Wed	Thu	Fri	Sat	Sun
Walking Step target: Steps done: Exertion rate:							
Strength* Minutes: Notes:							
Flexibility† Minutes: Notes:							
Balance* (Optional) Minutes: Notes:							

*Preferably three non-consecutive days
†Aim for at least three sessions per week

Six-week Exercise Plan – Week 4

	Mon	Tue	Wed	Thu	Fri	Sat	Sun
Walking Step target: Steps done: Exertion rate:							
Strength* Minutes: Notes:							
Flexibility† Minutes: Notes:							
Balance* (Optional) Minutes: Notes:							

*Preferably three non-consecutive days
†Aim for at least three sessions per week

Six-week Exercise Plan – Week 5

	Mon	Tue	Wed	Thu	Fri	Sat	Sun
Walking Step target: Steps done: Exertion rate:							
Strength* Minutes: Notes:							
Flexibility† Minutes: Notes:							
Balance* (Optional) Minutes: Notes:							

*Preferably three non-consecutive days
†Aim for at least three sessions per week

Six-week Exercise Plan – Week 6

Week 6	Mon	Tue	Wed	Thu	Fri	Sat	Sun
Walking Step target: Steps done: Exertion rate:							
Strength* Minutes: Notes:							
Flexibility† Minutes: Notes:							
Balance* (Optional) Minutes: Notes:							

*Preferably three non-consecutive days
†Aim for at least three sessions per week

Check Your Posture

Everyone talks about the importance of good posture. It is fundamental to the way you move your body and to your ability to progress successfully on the six-week exercise plan. With better posture you'll get more out of your exercises, become fitter and more energetic, and you'll look trimmer.

Having good posture is not just a case of standing up straight. In fact, as we go through life, getting our posture right can become more challenging. We accumulate a whole collection of muscle memories that shape how we stand, sit and walk. These little muscle memories can be quite difficult to change when you look at your body as a whole. However, when you break it down systematically to different sections, you can see how small improvements in positioning can change posture and your appearance, plus make a big impact on your exercise enjoyment.

Step-by-step Guide to Improving Your Posture

When examining your posture, there are six areas of the body to consider. Here is a step-by-step guide.

Step 1: Foot Position

The first step is to learn how to position your feet properly. This includes controlling the arch to ensure that the foot is not rolling in or out. It's quite common for the arches to flatten out and lose their ability to support the foot. This is most likely to happen to the longitudinal arch, which runs from your toes to the pad of your heel. If you stand with bare feet you should be able to get two fingers beneath the arch of your foot – if you can't, you probably have fallen arches. A fallen arch has a sneaky knock-on effect on the positioning of your whole leg. You will probably see that your knees roll in slightly. If you now try to lift the arch of your foot, you will see the knees come more in line above your ankles. To help you picture this, if you drew a line down the middle of your kneecap, it should extend down to your second toe. To help rectify fallen arches, perform toe curls. With bare feet, curl your toes 15–20 times on a carpet, imagining that you are trying to pick up a pencil.

Step 2: Weight Distribution

The second step is being aware of how you distribute your weight. You need to understand what it feels like when the weight is falling directly over your ankle. You can do this by gently rolling forward and backward on your feet until you find a comfortable middle position. This is the position where you are resting the weight neither on your toes nor on your ankles. Now rock slowly from side to side so you experience a similar shift laterally. Come to a central position again. The end result of steps one and two is that your weight is evenly distributed between your little toe, big toe and heel; and between these three points there should be a gently lifting of the arch of your foot between the heel pad and the ball of your foot.

Step 3: Knee Tracking

There should always be an imaginary line between the big and second toe, the centre of the knee and the centre of the hip. Once you have got the arch of your foot under control, as in steps one and two, you should find that your knee alignment takes care of itself.

Step 4: Pelvic Control

Pelvic control means there shouldn't be a shift in your hips and pelvic girdle as you take a stride. If you walk behind someone with poor pelvic control you will notice their hips swing or their upper body tilts from side to side with each step taken. One of the simplest ways to help correct poor pelvic control is to imagine you have a full glass of water resting on the top of each hip bone. As you walk or make any movement, your aim is to try and keep each glass full. Other useful ways to help retrain your pelvic control are pulling in your lower tummy muscles as if trying to do up a tight pair of trousers or skirt; or walking tall, extending through the crown of the head.

Step 5: Stabilizing Your Torso

Your torso – the thoracic and scapular region of the body – relates to your ribcage and shoulder girdle. Once your pelvic control has improved, you will find that the stabilization of your upper torso should automatically get better. Remember, though, to be aware of the tendency to elevate and hunch the shoulders. This can be caused by years of bags on shoulders, balancing the telephone receiver between your chin and your shoulder, as well as cold weather. Practise lengthening your shoulders down to the floor and stretching your fingertips to the ground, whilst stretching the crown of your head and lengthening through the back of the neck at the same time. Try to create as much of a gap between these two points as possible.

> Think elegant and distinguished and your body will naturally find it easier to fall into the right position.

Step 6: Centring the Head

The final step is to centre the head, front to back and side to side. As we age, there is a tendency for the chin to jut out. This is likely to occur in situations such as staring at a computer screen and reaching forward to help someone or hear someone clearly. When we are tired, there is also a tendency towards tilting the head to the side. All these create muscle imbalances that can have a knock-on effect throughout the body. Try to think of your chin and ears being parallel to the floor.

Practising these postural exercises in front of a full-length mirror, wearing your underwear or shorts and a fitted top, will help give you visual reference points. As your body starts to understand and gain a memory of how correct posture feels, you will be able to put these little reminders into practice in your exercise programmes and throughout your day.

Exercising Safely

Most people can and should exercise. However, you should consult your GP before exercising if any of the following apply to you:

- You have a medical condition such as elevated blood glucose or cholesterol or high blood pressure.
- You have an injury. You may need to wait for it to heal – listen to your body and your doctor.
- You have a cardiac, pulmonary or metabolic disease. You may exercise, but only after seeing your doctor and then starting in a supervised environment.

Here are some tips for exercising safely:

- Start slowly in moderation. For endurance exercise, simply walk a little further than you normally do and progress to walking further and faster as the weeks and months pass. For strength exercise, lift a weight you are accustomed to lifting but do it more times than usual, progressing gradually to lifting it 15 times.
- To start endurance or strength exercises at a vigorous level, see your doctor first and then consult an exercise professional for screening tests and programme advice.
- You should always be able to catch your breath and speak comfortably while exercising.
- You should sense effort, maybe some discomfort, but never pain.
- Learn to use the Perceived Exertion Rate scale (see page 116).
- Always remember to warm up (start slowly) and cool down (stop gradually) (see page 118).

7 The Six-week Eating Plan

Diets don't work – *you* work.

This chapter contains all the information you need to follow the six-week eating plan, as well as lots of tips to help you continue your efforts after you have completed the programme. There is information on the important nutrients you need to minimize ageing and boost vitality. Not only will you look and feel healthier, you will lose weight too.

How the Eating Plan Works

- The eating plan is based on 'optimum nutrition calorie restriction' (see Chapter 4). You will be consuming 1,400–1,700 calories a day.
- It applies the highly successful Carb Curfew approach (see Chapter 4), so you'll be avoiding bread, pasta, rice and potatoes with your evening meal.
- Nutrient-dense foods such as fruits, vegetables, beans and legumes form the mainstay of your diet.
- It follows a low-to-moderate GI style of eating, helping to boost your energy and keep hunger at bay.

- Protein sources are still vitally important, but the focus is on leaner cuts of meat and fish.
- It's rich in vitamin E and healthy omega-3 fatty acids, such as those found in oily fish, walnuts and flaxseeds, which enhance insulin sensitivity. You'll enjoy good sources of essential fats from unsalted nuts, such as pecans, walnuts and almonds, and from salad dressings using plant oils such as canola and extra virgin olive oil.
- Foods high in trans fats and partially hydrogenated oils, such as those found in margarines and many processed foods, are avoided.
- Butter, saturated fats and fried foods are minimized and replaced with healthy heart alternatives, such as avocado, olive oil and flaxseed oil.
- You can still enjoy beverages such as tea and alcohol, but you'll be able to boost your health quota by drinking the right ones in the right amounts.
- It is naturally low in sodium.
- You'll find ways to detect hidden calorie saboteurs, such as those found in many drinks and condiments.

I have designed menu plans for six weeks so you can easily get all the nutrients you need. Each menu plan is calorie counted and will keep your energy levels balanced. You'll find the menu plans on pages 197–209.

The Macronutrients You Need

Foods contain six classes of nutrients: carbohydrates, fats, proteins, vitamins, minerals and water. Only carbohydrates, fats and proteins provide the body with energy. These are called 'macronutrients'. Although vitamins and minerals provide no calories, they are essential for the breakdown of macronutrients and are termed 'micronutrients'.

Carbohydrates

Carbohydrates form the backbone of our diet. Foods rich in carbohydrates include:

- Fruits
- Vegetables
- Sugary foods like biscuits and cakes
- Starchy foods like potatoes, rice and bread

Carbohydrate-rich foods supply the body with its primary source of fuel – glucose, a type of sugar, which the body can easily use and transport. Glucose can also be stored in the muscles as glycogen, and is the main source of fuel for the nervous system and brain. Carbohydrates must be present for the body to be able to burn fat; however, any excess calories from carbohydrates will be converted to and stored as body fat in the fat cells.

Traditionally, carbohydrates have been described as either 'simple' or 'complex'. Simple carbohydrates are found in products made from refined sugar, such as biscuits and cakes, and in fruit. The body can quickly convert these simple sugars to glucose for energy. Complex carbohydrates are found in starchy foods such as bread and pasta. It takes the body longer to convert these carbohydrates to glucose.

The key issue for health and weight management, however, is not the classification of sugars but how the body handles each specific sugar. What's important is how rapidly a carbohydrate is absorbed into your bloodstream. When you eat a sugary snack, the body deals with the sudden carbohydrate rush by 'flooding' the bloodstream with insulin. A dramatic rise in insulin levels causes two responses:

1. Lowering of blood sugar beyond normal levels, known as hypoglycaemia
2. Increased fat storage

Have you ever eaten something sweet to give yourself an energy boost and, 30 minutes later, felt more tired than you were before? That's the hypogly-caemic backlash response, which may also trigger you reaching for another sweet snack to boost blood sugar levels again.

The Glycaemic Index

More recently, carbohydrates have been classified according to the Glycaemic Index (GI). This rating is a more useful tool, as it tells us how quickly a partic-ular carbohydrate will raise blood sugar levels.

Several factors can influence the GI of a food, including:

- Its fat and protein content
- How much it has been processed
- The amount of dietary fibre it contains
- Whether it is solid or liquid

- Low-GI foods have a rating of less than 55
- Moderate-GI foods have a rating of 56–69
- High-GI foods have a rating of 70 or more

Low-GI diets have become popular recently as they are thought to maintain energy levels through stabilizing insulin. In general, non-starchy vegetables, fruits, legumes and nuts have a low GI, and these foods form the basis of your six-week eating plan.

The Glycaemic Load

One drawback of the Glycaemic Index is that the rating of a particular food doesn't take into account the amount of the food you eat. To do this accurately you need to establish the Glycaemic Load (GL). The GL is the GI divided by 100 and then multiplied by the available carbohydrate content of the food.

Consuming a large portion of a high-GI food will bring about a greater glycaemic response than eating a small amount. For example, both potatoes and carrots are high-GI foods but we would typically eat only half a cup of carrots (one serving) whereas we could easily eat 1–3 large spoonfuls of mashed potatoes. You would get a much higher GL from the potatoes than the carrots because you are eating more grams of carbohydrates. The GI Walking Diet menu ideas take account of both the GI and GL, but when applying the principle to yourself you may need to be aware of the GL. Eating a variety of foods of low-to-moderate GI rating will help. Remember, there is no magic food, so enjoy following the six-week menu plan.

Protein

Essential for tissue repair, maintenance and growth, protein is part of every cell in the body. It plays such an important role in repairing the body that it is much harder for the body to store excess protein as body fat.

Proteins are made up of chains of amino acids. There are hundreds of amino acids in nature, but only 20 are important to humans. Of these, eight are considered 'essential', as we cannot manufacture them in the body, and therefore need to get them from the foods we eat.

Protein can be divided into two groups:

- Dairy products, including milk, cheese and yoghurt
- Non-dairy sources, including meat, fish, nuts, seeds, eggs, pulses and beans

If you eat a variety of foods, it is not difficult to get all your essential amino acids. However, if you are a vegetarian or vegan, you need to take a little more care with your protein intake. Plant protein sources, such as legumes, nuts and seeds, tend not to contain all the essential amino acids. It is therefore important that vegetarians get a good mix of plant proteins to obtain all the essential amino acids. The six-week eating plan has a variety of vegetarian recipes as well as nutrient-dense snacks featuring nuts and seeds.

Dietary Fat

A lot has been written about dietary fat, so much so that it can be confusing trying to distinguish the good stuff from the bad stuff. The GI Walking Diet is packed with good fats while minimizing bad fats. But what exactly is good fat and bad fat?

Saturated and Unsaturated Fats

Dietary fat is largely made up of fatty acids. There are two main types of fatty acid: saturated and unsaturated. Although both types are present in fat, dietary fats are categorized based on the predominant fat. Saturated fats are considered the least healthy of the two due to their negative effects on cholesterol levels. Most unsaturated fats are considered healthier than saturated fats. These healthier alternatives are chiefly made up of cis fatty acids, which function optimally in the body. Some unsaturated fats, however, are primarily made up of trans fatty acids. These have a chemical formation closer to that of saturated fat, and have also been shown to be detrimental to our health.

Trans Fats, the New Bad Fats

Recent studies have indicated that unsaturated fat containing trans fatty acids – known as trans fats – may be just as harmful to health as saturated fat. Trans fats have been shown to interfere with the way healthy cis fatty acids work in the body, impairing vital functions such as immunity, cell membrane development and enzyme activity. Trans fats can specifically affect the function of two of the most important cis fatty acids: linoleic acid and linolenic acid. These two cis fatty acids are considered essential since they can be obtained only through dietary sources like plant oils.

There is strong scientific evidence linking trans fats to an increased risk of cardiovascular disease. Trans fats have been shown to increase levels of 'bad' LDL cholesterol and decrease 'good' HDL cholesterol. They have also been linked to certain cancers. Additionally, a diet with a high number of calories from trans fats has been shown to contribute to an increased waist circumference, one measure you most definitely do not want to increase. And a large study of women found that a slight increase in trans fat consumption increased the risk of developing diabetes.

Trans fats are found in both animal and plant sources. The vast majority of trans fats in our diet come from processed plant oils. Healthy plant oils undergo a process known as hydrogenation, which changes their make-up from a good fat to an unhealthy one. In the hydrogenation process, the oils are heated to a very high temperature in the presence of hydrogen, causing some of the unsaturated cis fatty acids to become saturated fatty acids, and some to be transformed into trans fats. The longer the oil is hydrogenated, the more saturated and solid the fat becomes. Margarine bought in a block is harder than tub margarine because it has undergone a longer hydrogenation process, and therefore contains more saturated and trans fats.

Ironically, in the 1960s and 1970s, foods made from hydrogenated vegetable oils were viewed as healthy alternatives to butter and lard. Products like margarine were praised because they contained little or no cholesterol and less saturated fat than butter and lard. At the time, all unsaturated fatty acids were thought to function in the body in the same way, regardless of whether they were in the cis or trans formation. It wasn't until the 1990s that substantial evidence began to accumulate about the harmful effects trans fats have on our health.

Despite these discoveries, the quantity of trans fats in our diets has continued to increase. Manufacturers rely on the hydrogenation process to prevent oils from becoming rancid, thus improving the product's shelf life. Many of your favourite commercial cakes, biscuits and other baked snack products will be high in these unhealthy trans fats. You may be surprised at the number of common foods that are high in trans fats, and how easy it is to consume this type of fat unwittingly over the course of a day.

Where Your Trans Fats Sneak In

Even if you think you don't consume that much processed food, you may be surprised at how much can sneak into your diet. This applies to the whole family, including young children, who are particularly attracted to snack foods. Take the following daily menu as a typical example:

- **Breakfast:** two slices of toasted bread made with partially hydrogenated vegetable oil spread with two teaspoons of soft margarine and chocolate spread (3g trans fat)
- **Morning snack:** cup of tea and one large baked biscuit (3g trans fat)
- **Lunch:** a cup of soup with four dry crackers (1g trans fat)
- **Afternoon snack:** crackers, cheese and grapes (2g trans fat)
- **Dinner:** small steak, chips and a bread roll (3.5g trans fat)

This modest daily menu contains a whopping 12.5g of trans fat! To put this into perspective, remember that for someone eating approximately 1,700 calories a day, 12.5g of trans fat amounts to nearly 6 per cent of their total calories.

Trans fats are commonly found in the following ready-to-eat and processed foods:

- Biscuits
- Flavoured instant coffee powders
- Boxed convenience foods such as instant noodles
- Dry food supplements
- Energy bars
- Frozen chicken pies
- Bread
- Breaded scampi

- Cake and pancake mixes
- Frozen pizza
- Cakes, muffins, doughnuts and icings
- Frozen waffles and pancakes
- Fruit pies made with pastry
- Chips
- Higher-fat breakfast cereals like crunchy muesli
- Margarines (solid block more than tub)

Reducing your Trans Fat Intake

By following the GI Walking Diet, you will automatically keep your intake of trans fats low. If, however, you prefer to follow a more flexible eating plan in conjunction with your exercise programme, here are some tips to decrease your daily intake of trans fats:

- Lower total dietary fat intake by choosing a diet rich in fruits, vegetables, legumes, low-fat dairy products and grilled lean meats and fish Most people eat much more saturated fat than trans fat each day, so limiting total fat intake will decrease the amount of unhealthy saturated and trans fats in the diet.
- Replace 'hard block' fats like margarine with salad oils, such as extra virgin olive oil. When baking your own breads, cakes and pancakes, use liquid vegetable oil instead of shortening. Substitute pastry and suet toppings on pies and casseroles with inventive vegetable options. Look at the recipes in Chapter 8 for some imaginative and healthy ideas.
- At restaurants, dip your bread in extra virgin olive oil instead of spreading it with butter or block margarine, or use a trans fats-free margarine, peanut butter or other nut butter. Almond butter is particularly enjoyable on wholemeal toast. Look for these products in supermarkets and health-food shops.

- Avoid deep-fried foods whenever possible, especially when eating out at restaurants. Snacks such as chips, doughnuts and croissants are particularly loaded with trans fats. Your local chip shop may tell you they only cook in vegetable oil, but think of the number of times that oil gets reheated, creating trans fats in the process.
- Look for the term 'partially hydrogenated vegetable oil' on food labels. The higher up such an oil appears on the list of ingredients, the more trans fats are likely to be in the food. Don't be fooled by a phrase such as 'No cholesterol, containing all vegetable oil' as this doesn't mean the product is free of trans fats. American-sourced products are now commonplace in our shops – their labels are often marked more clearly than UK ones.

Dietary Fibre

Dietary fibre is the indigestible part of our food that gives bulk to our digestive system. There are two types of dietary fibre:

- **Soluble fibre.** This type of fibre dissolves in water and forms a gel. Found in fruits, vegetables, legumes and oat bran, it helps reduce cholesterol when eaten as part of a diet low in saturated fat. Soluble fat can also help control blood sugar.
- **Insoluble fibre.** This fibre cannot dissolve in water, but instead absorbs water as it passes through the body. Found in fruits, vegetables, whole grains and wheat bran, it adds faecal bulk and helps speed up the rate at which food passes through the digestive system.

It's difficult to separate the effects of fibre from the foods themselves because food contains other nutrients and phytochemicals that protect against chronic diseases and obesity. Nevertheless, a recent study in the *American Journal of Clinical Nutrition* gives fibre most of the credit for cardiovascular protection.

Whole grains or cereal fibre can lower your risk of heart disease by 30 per cent.

Extensive research has found that a high intake of dietary fibre – specifically from cereals and beans – is linked to increased life span. Have a look at the Fibre Fueller Cereal recipe on page 220 for a delicious high-fibre breakfast. If you aren't keen on the taste of high-fibre cereals, try mixing it with another lower-fibre cereal with a taste you like. You'll find many other fibre-rich recipes in Chapter 8. For example:

- Crunchy Pear and Yoghurt Energizer for breakfast (page 223)
- Stuffed Pitta Bread with Falafel (page 231)
- Lentil Soup with Spinach (page 245)
- Grilled Steak with Roasted Beetroot and Creamed Spinach (page 272) (the beetroot and spinach provide the fibre)
- Vegetable Stew (page 289)
- Salad of Turkey Breast with Lentils, Mushrooms and Watercress (page 260)
- Hotpot with Haricot or Cannellini Beans (page 291)

The Micronutrients You Need

The following vitamins and minerals are especially important in the GI Walking Diet.

Vitamin A

Why it's Important

Vitamin A protects and maintains our eyes and the linings of our respiratory, urinary and intestinal tracts as well as the elasticity of our skin. Eating a diet rich in vitamin A has been shown to lower the risk of developing age-related macular degeneration, a leading cause of blindness, by 36 per cent.

How Do I Get It?

Retinol or preformed vitamin A is abundant in liver, eggs and fortified foods such as milk. The dark pigments found in colourful fruits and vegetables are especially rich in the carotenoids, which the body converts to vitamin A. Sweet potato, pumpkin, squash, carrots and kale are especially rich.

Recipes to Try

- Pumpkin and Pancetta Pasta (page 234)
- Vegetable Stew (page 289)
- Minestrone Soup (page 282)
- Thai-style Steamed Hake with Spinach and Gingered Carrots (page 280)
- Healthy Eggs Benedict (page 242)

Vitamin C

Why it's Important

Vitamin C literally holds us together. It's necessary for the synthesis of collagen, the 'glue' that binds our ligaments, bones, blood vessels and skin. It also plays a role in making brain chemicals, breaking down cholesterol and neutralizing those highly reactive free radicals. There is also some evidence that vitamin C may protect against infections that can trigger arthritis.

How Do I Get It?

Orange juice is a simple and easy option. Eating a whole orange will give you some fibre too. Other options are kiwi fruit, raw red or green pepper, broccoli, strawberries, Brussels sprouts and cantaloupe melon.

Recipes to Try

- Winter Vegetable Bake (page 292)
- Crab Cakes with Crunchy Warm Coleslaw (page 236) (the vitamin C is found in the cabbage)
- Chicken, Avocado, Walnut and Watercress Salad in Granary Bread (page 230)
- Estela's One Pan Easy Supper (page 258)
- Cinnamon-poached Fruit (page 302)

Vitamin E

Why it's Important

Vitamin E is an antioxidant, disarming free radicals and protecting cells from damage. It also plays a role in immunity; research suggests it may even help prevent the common cold. Studies have shown that people with the highest daily intake of vitamin E have a significantly lower risk of Parkinson's disease.

How Do I Get It?

Vitamin E can be found in small amounts in a lot of foods, so you have to work quite hard to get the right amount. It also tends to be found in energy-dense foods, so getting an adequate supply can come with a high-calorie price tag. Spinach, almonds, sunflower oil and seeds and avocado are good sources.

> Don't feel guilty about dressing a salad with oil as evidence suggests a little fat helps you absorb the nutrients from the vegetables, and ferries vitamin E into your bloodstream.

Recipes to Try

- Chicken and Spinach Salad (page 248)
- Snack on 30g/1oz almonds (about 24 nuts)
- 1 Ryvita cracker with avocado
- Morning Super-nutrient Energizer Porridge (page 213)
- Nutty-topped Muffin with Fruit Salad (page 213)
- Chinese Chicken Noodle Salad with Toasted Almonds (page 240)
- Chicken, Avocado, Walnut and Watercress Salad in Granary Bread (page 230)

Selenium

Why it's Important

Selenium protects body tissues against oxidative damage, radiation and pollution. It's important for the efficient functioning of the immune system and liver, and it can help protect against heart and circulatory diseases. It is also believed to protect against some cancers.

How Do I Get It?

Selenium sources include meat, shellfish, brazil nuts, whole-grain cereals and dairy products. The amount provided by vegetables varies according to the selenium content of soil. Barley and brown rice are also good sources of selenium.

Recipes to Try

- Seafood Chowder (page 274)
- Chinese Chicken Noodle Salad with Toasted Almonds (page 240)
- Nutty Chicken Pitta Pockets (page 229)
- Roast Trout Fillets with Bacon and Green Beans (page 276)
- Grilled Tuna Steak with Gremolata and a Mixed Bean Salad (page 278)

Magnesium and Potassium

Why They're Important

A diet high in potassium and low in sodium protects against a number of diseases and can be therapeutic in cases of high blood pressure. Numerous studies have shown that sodium restriction alone does not improve blood pressure control in most people – it must be accompanied by a high potassium intake. Studies have also linked these minerals with sometimes dramatic protection from diabetes, heart disease and osteoporosis.

How Do I Get Them?

Drink milk, eat pumpkin seeds, add bran to your breakfast cereal and don't forget cooked spinach. For magnesium, eat green vegetables, nuts and whole grains. For potassium, eat sweet potatoes, white potatoes, white beans and bananas.

Recipes to Try

- Banana Muffins (page 300)
- Shepherd's Pie with Carb Curfew Crust (page 264)
- Vegetable Stew (page 289)
- Hot Pot with Haricot or Cannellini Beans (page 291)
- Chicken and Spinach Salad (page 248)
- Braised Chicken and Fennel with Leeks and Green Beans (page 256)

Calcium

Why it's Important

Calcium provides the building material for your teeth and bones. The mineral also plays a role in the constriction and relaxation of your blood vessels, contributing to healthy blood pressure. Newer studies even suggest that a higher intake of calcium may reduce your risk of colorectal cancer. A review of 10 studies involving more than half a million people, published in 2004 by Harvard researchers, found that drinking milk seems to protect against this leading cause of cancer death. Low calcium intakes are now also associated with weight gain, although the exact mechanism is still to be confirmed.

How Do I Get It?

The best way is to drink fat-free or low-fat milk daily. Ideally, choose a milk that is also rich in vitamin D, which your body needs for optimal calcium absorption. Low vitamin D is a risk factor for osteoporosis. If you don't get enough D – even if you are getting enough calcium – your body will start pulling calcium from your bones to keep blood levels normal. Other calcium-rich sources are fat-free yoghurt, low-fat cheese and fortified orange juice.

Recipes to Try

You'll notice that many of the breakfasts include a glass of milk or calcium-fortified fruit juice.

The Anutrients You Need

'Anutrient' is the term for an important group of antioxidants essential to health. Antioxidants are important in the fight against ageing as they directly tackle free radicals, changing their chemical structure and rendering them harmless. Consuming adequate amounts of all the anutrients is important as each works in a different way and at a different site. Some work within the cells while others combat the free radicals directly within your bloodstream, in the blood serum. There are three types of antioxidant:

- Food-based vitamin antioxidants include vitamins A, C and E. These tend to focus their attack against free radicals in the cells.
- Phytochemicals include carotene, flavonoids and allium. They are also found in foods and have similar antioxidant properties to vitamins A, C and E, attacking the free radicals in the cells but also enhancing important enzymes and boosting the immune system. The following table gives you a full list of these phytochemicals and their food sources.
- The mineral selenium functions like an antioxidant, specifically in the blood serum.

Anutrient	Health Benefits	Food Sources	Recipes to Try
Allium compounds	Lower cholesterol levels, anti-tumour properties	Garlic and onions	Braised Chicken and Fennel with Leeks and Green Beans (p.256)
Carotenes	Antioxidant, enhance immune system, anti-cancer properties	Darkly coloured vegetables such as carrots, squash, kale, spinach; apricots and citrus fruits	Minestrone Soup (p.282) Pumpkin and Pancetta Pasta (p.234)
Coumarins	Anti-tumour properties, immune system enhancement, stimulates antioxidants	Carrots, celery, beets and citrus fruits	Grilled Steak with Roasted Beetroot and Creamed Spinach (p.272)
Dithiol-thiones	Block the reaction of cancer-causing compounds within our cells	Cabbage-family vegetables	Minestrone Soup (p.282)
Flavonoids	Antioxidant, antiviral and anti-inflammatory properties	Fruits, especially cherries and blueberries; vegetables including tomatoes, peppers	Estela's One Pan Supper (p.258)

Anutrient	Health Benefits	Food Sources	Recipes to Try
Glucosin-olates & Indoles	Stimulate enzymes that detoxify cancer-causing compounds	Cabbage, Brussels sprouts, radishes, kale, mustard greens	Thai-style Steamed Hake with Spinach and Gingered Carrots (p.280)
Isothio-cyanates & Thio-cyanates	Inhibit damage to genetic material (DNA)	Cabbage-family vegetables	Minestrone Soup (p.282)
Limonoids	Protect against cancer	Citrus fruits	Cinnamon-poached Fruit (p.302)
Phthalides	Stimulate detoxification enzymes	Parsley, carrots, celery	Grilled Tuna Steak with Gremolata and a Mixed Bean Salad (p.278)
Sterols	Block the production of cancer-causing compounds	Soya products, whole grains, cucumber, cabbage-family veg, squash and pumpkin	Winter Vegetable Soup or Bake (p.292)

Drinks

Tea Time!

If everything is starting to sound a bit too healthy and you are feeling you may have to give up your afternoon cuppa and slice of cake, don't worry!

> You can still enjoy your favourite cuppa, confident you are doing yourself some good at the same time.

Tea is increasingly being hailed by scientists for its ability to ward off common diseases such as osteoporosis, heart attacks, Parkinson's disease and even gum disease. Tea does contain some caffeine, but some studies have shown that caffeine may actually reduce muscle pain during exercise and play a role in preventing cancer. If you're wary of caffeine, caffeine-free varieties of tea are readily available. Here are some of the colourful teas you can now choose from and enjoy with your afternoon snack.

- **Red tea.** This herbal variety, also known as rooibos tea, is naturally caffeine-free. Made from the stems and twigs of the rooibos plant, it is typically sold as loose tea, although it is available in tea bags. It has a fruity, slightly sweet flavour and contains many disease-fighting antioxidants, such as polyphenols and flavonoids.
- **Green tea.** Because green tea is one of the least processed teas, it contains more antioxidants than most other teas. Available in caffeinated and decaffeinated versions, green tea has long been used to treat cold symptoms such as coughs and sore throats. It is also thought to help fight certain cancers, particularly of the prostate, stomach and oesophagus. And since green

tea increases metabolic rate, scientists are now studying its potential for weight control.

- **Black tea.** Although the most processed of the bunch, black tea is still thought to confer health benefits. It has been reported to lower cancer risk, decrease 'bad' LDL cholesterol levels and lower the risk of heart disease. It is widely available in tea bags or as loose tea, and can be decaffeinated or not.
- **White tea.** Although less studied than other varieties, white tea is also thought to have health benefits. Unfortunately, it can be difficult to find and you may have to pay dearly for it. It can be purchased in bags or in loose form and is the least processed tea on the market.
- **Brassica Tea.** This brand-name tea is partly derived from broccoli sprouts, but the broccoli flavour can't be detected! It also contains green, black and red tea. Like broccoli, Brassica Tea is high in antioxidants. Developed by researchers from Johns Hopkins University, it may help prevent cancer and macular degeneration eye disease.

Alcohol

In my research for this book, I found that alcohol was an important part of the majority of respondents' lives. It is true that some studies indicate that enjoying two alcoholic drinks a day, especially antioxidant-rich red wine, may confer cardiovascular benefits. However, a recent study found that heavy alcohol use weakens bones and may increase the risk of breast cancer.

Many people forget that alcohol is a considerable source of calories. A standard beer contains 190 calories, and most mixed drinks weigh in at about 80–100 calories each. So do enjoy your alcohol but go easy on it.

Water, Juice and Milk

Being properly hydrated has a positive effect on your energy levels. In later life, our thirst mechanism can become suppressed as we get accustomed to not drinking enough water and hydrating ourselves. In this situation, the brain is unable to make a clear thirst signal to the body, and we often interpret it as a message to eat.

Staying hydrated is important and will affect your enjoyment of the GI Walking Diet, but you don't have to drink masses of water. You can get your hydration from other nutrient-dense sources such as low-fat milk and natural fruit juices. You will see that the menu plans list juices and milk in many of the meals. These not only provide hydration but are also a source of vitamins and essential calcium. I always advise diluting your fruit juice with a little water as this makes it easier for the body to absorb, and the natural sugars will cause less of a blood sugar 'spike'. In between meals, try to drink small glasses of water, little and often.

The Menu Plans

The following menu plans give options for breakfast, lunch and dinner for six weeks. For your daily snack, please see the list on page 303. For more information about using these menu plans, see Chapter 4, page 80. In Chapter 8 you'll find all the delicious recipes you can enjoy on the GI Walking Diet.

Where no drink is specified, opt for water.

Week 1

Day 1
Breakfast: Classic Porridge with Fruit, Yoghurt and Nuts (p.211)
Lunch: Pear, Gorgonzola and Walnut Salad (p.227). Glass of semi-skimmed milk. Piece of fruit
Dinner: Braised Chicken and Fennel with Leeks and Green Beans (p.256). Piece of fruit

Day 2
Breakfast: Fibre Fueller Cereal (p.220)
Lunch: Herby Cheese Field Mushrooms (p.232). Glass of fruit juice
Dinner: Grilled Tuna Steak with Gremolata and a Mixed Bean Salad (p.278). Cinnamon-poached Fruit (p.302)

Day 3
Breakfast: Nutty-topped Muffin with Fruit Salad (p.213)
Lunch: Pumpkin and Pancetta Pasta (p.234). Small green salad
Dinner: Winter Vegetable Bake (p.292). Mixed Berry Salad with Low-fat Creamy Dressing (p.298)

Day 4
Breakfast: Super-healthy Egg White Omelette (p.212)
Lunch: Country Vegetable Soup with Cheese Toast (p.228). Glass of milk
Dinner: Stir-fried Beef with Grilled Asparagus and a Lemon and Thyme Dressing (p.270). Mixed Berry Salad with Low-fat Creamy Dressing (p.298)

Day 5

Breakfast: Fruity Wholemeal Toast (p.216)

Lunch: Cottage Cheese, Peach and Walnut Salad (p.226)

Dinner: Lamb Chops with Mixed Peppercorns (p.266). Small green salad with olive oil dressing. Piece of fruit

Day 6

Breakfast: Morning Super-nutrient Energizer Porridge (p.213)

Lunch: Chicken, Avocado, Walnut and Watercress Salad in Granary Bread (p.230). Glass of orange juice

Dinner: Shepherd's Pie with Carb Curfew Crust (p.264). Fresh fruit salad

Day 7

Breakfast: Healthy Cooked Breakfast (p.224)

Lunch: Roast Chicken with Lemon and Tarragon (p.254). Low-fat New York Lemon Cheesecake with Raspberries (p.296)

Dinner: Seafood Chowder (p.274). Cinnamon-poached Fruit (p.302)

Week 2

Day 1

Breakfast: Morning Super-nutrient Energizer Porridge (p.213)

Lunch: Chicken, Avocado, Walnut and Watercress Salad in Granary Bread (p.230). Glass of fruit juice

Dinner: Lamb Stew with Ginger and Mint, with Wilted Spinach Leaves (p.268). Mixed Berry Salad with Low-fat Creamy Dressing (p.298)

Day 2

Breakfast: Nutty-topped Muffin with Fruit Salad (p.213)

Lunch: Salmon Pâté with Watercress Salad (p.252). Glass of fruit juice

Dinner: Grilled Pork Steaks with Spicy Sweetcorn Salsa (p.262). Cinnamon-poached Fruit (p.302)

Day 3

Breakfast: Cereal and Fruit Juice (p.222)

Lunch: Omelette with Tomato and Fresh Basil. Small green salad with olive oil dressing (p.238)

Dinner: Seafood Chowder (p.274). Estela's One Pan Easy Supper (p.258). Piece of fruit

Day 4

Breakfast: Fibre Fueller Cereal (p.220)

Lunch: Lentil Soup with Spinach (p.245). Glass of tomato juice

Dinner: Shepherd's Pie with Carb Curfew Crust (p.264). Cinnamon-poached Fruit (p.302) with natural yoghurt

Day 5

Breakfast: Fruity Toasted Teacake (p.217)

Lunch: Salad of Spinach, Feta, Mint and Pine Nuts (p.250). Banana Muffin (p.300). Glass of milk

Dinner: Thai-style Steamed Hake with Spinach and Gingered Carrots (p.280). Fresh Fruit Salad

Day 6

Breakfast: Savoury Scrambled Eggs (p.212)

Lunch: Chicken Liver Pâté (p.246) with Melba toast. Crab Cakes with Crunchy Warm Coleslaw (p.236)

Dinner: Hotpot with Haricot or Cannellini Beans (p.291). Piece of fruit

Day 7

Breakfast: Nutty-topped Muffin with Fruit Salad (p.213)

Lunch: Grilled Steak with Roasted Beetroot and Creamed Spinach (p.272) Mixed Berry Salad with Low-fat Creamy Dressing (p.298)

Dinner: French-style Chicken Soup (p.288). Cinnamon-poached Fruit (p.302)

Week 3

Day 1
Breakfast: Cereal and Fruit Juice (p.222)
Lunch: Chicken Liver Pâté (p.246), toast and salad. Glass of orange juice
Dinner: Roast Trout Fillets with Bacon and Green Beans (p.276). Piece of fruit and low-fat natural yoghurt sprinkled with chopped walnuts

Day 2
Breakfast: Morning Super-nutrient Energizer Porridge (p.213)
Lunch: Healthy Eggs Benedict (p.242). Glass of milk
Dinner: Stir-fried Beef with Grilled Asparagus and a Lemon and Thyme Dressing (p.270). Cinnamon-poached Fruit (p.302)

Day 3
Breakfast: Fibre Fueller Cereal (p.220)
Lunch: Chicken and Spinach Salad (p.248). Glass of orange juice
Dinner: Hotpot with Haricot or Cannellini Beans (p.291). Two cubes dark high-cocoa chocolate

Day 4
Breakfast: Nutty-topped Muffin with Fruit Salad (p.213)
Lunch: Stuffed Pitta Bread with Falafel (p.231). Glass of milk
Dinner: Grilled Tuna Steak with Gremolata and a Mixed Bean Salad (p.278). Piece of fruit

Day 5

Breakfast: Boiled Egg and Soldiers (p.221)

Lunch: Chinese Chicken Noodle Salad with Toasted Almonds (p.240)

Dinner: Shepherd's Pie with Carb Curfew Crust (p.264). Small green salad with olive oil dressing. Natural low-fat yoghurt

Day 6

Breakfast: Fruity Wholemeal Toast (p.216)

Lunch: Melon and Parma Ham with Mint Vinaigrette (p.249). Glass of milk. Two cubes dark high-cocoa chocolate

Dinner: Braised Chicken and Fennel with Leeks and Green Beans (p.256) Cinnamon-poached Fruit (p.302)

Day 7

Breakfast: Baked Stuffed Breakfast Apple (p.214)

Lunch: Lamb Chops with Mixed Peppercorns (p.266). Low-fat New York Lemon Cheesecake with Raspberries (p.296)

Dinner: Salad of Turkey Breast with Lentils, Mushrooms and Watercress (p.260). Piece of fruit

Week 4

Day 1

Breakfast: Fibre Fueller Cereal (p.220)

Lunch: Herby Cheese Field Mushrooms (p.232). Glass of fruit juice

Dinner: Roast Trout Fillets with Bacon and Green Beans (p.276). Mixed Berry Salad with Low-fat Creamy Dressing (p.298)

Day 2

Breakfast: Cereal and Fruit Juice (p.222)

Lunch: Melon and Parma Ham with Mint Vinaigrette (p.249). Piece of fruit

Dinner: Hotpot with Haricot or Cannellini Beans (p.291). Natural low-fat yoghurt with handful of chopped almonds

Day 3

Breakfast: Fruity Wholemeal Toast (p.216)

Lunch: Omelette with Tomato and Fresh Basil (p.238). Natural low-fat yoghurt with handful of chopped almonds

Dinner: Estela's One Pan Easy Supper (p.258). Small green salad with olive oil dressing. Two cubes dark high-cocoa chocolate

Day 4

Breakfast: Crunchy Pear and Yoghurt Energizer (p.223)

Lunch: Lentil Soup with Spinach (p.245). Glass of orange juice

Dinner: Stir-fried Beef with Grilled Asparagus and a Lemon and Thyme Dressing (p.270). Piece of fruit

Day 5

Breakfast: Savoury Cheese Toast (p.215)

Lunch: Nutty Chicken Pitta Pockets (p.229). Glass of milk

Dinner: Vegetable Stew (p.289). Cinnamon-poached Fruit (p.302) sprinkled with handful of chopped almonds or walnuts

Day 6

Breakfast: Fibre Fueller Cereal (p.220)

Lunch: Stuffed Pitta Bread with Falafel (p.231). Glass of orange juice

Dinner: Thai-style Chicken Soup (p.287). Salad of Spinach, Feta, Mint and Pine Nuts (p.250). Piece of fruit

Day 7

Breakfast: Boiled Egg and Soldiers (p.221)

Lunch: Grilled Steak with Roasted Beetroot and Creamed Spinach (p.272) Two cubes dark high-cocoa chocolate

Dinner: Winter Vegetable Soup (p.292). Cinnamon-poached Fruit (p.302)

Week 5

Day 1
Breakfast: Cereal and Fruit Juice (p.222)
Lunch: Chicken Liver Pâté (p.246), toast and salad. Piece of fruit
Dinner: Winter Vegetable Bake (p.292). Mixed Berry Salad with Low-fat
Creamy Dressing (p.298)

Day 2
Breakfast: Boiled Egg and Soldiers (p.221)
Lunch: Lentil Soup with Spinach (p.245). Glass of orange juice
Dinner: Braised Chicken and Fennel with Leeks and Green Beans (p.256).
Mixed Berry Salad with Low-fat Creamy Dressing (p.298)

Day 3
Breakfast: Fibre Fueller Cereal (p.220)
Lunch: Salad of Spinach, Feta, Mint and Pine Nuts (p.250). Glass of fruit juice
Dinner: Grilled Tuna Steak with Gremolata and a Mixed Bean Salad (p.278)
Cinnamon-poached Fruit (p.302)

Day 4
Breakfast: Morning Super-nutrient Energizer Porridge (p.213)
Lunch: Cottage Cheese, Peach and Walnut Salad (p.226). Glass of fruit juice.
Dinner: Shepherd's Pie with Carb Curfew Crust (p.264), steamed peas and
carrots. Natural yoghurt with sprinkling of walnuts

Day 5

Breakfast: Savoury Cheese Toast (p.215)

Lunch: Salmon Pâté with Watercress Salad (p.252). Glass of orange juice

Dinner: Minestrone Soup (p.282). Melon and Parma Ham with Mint Vinaigrette (p.249)

Day 6

Breakfast: Baked Stuffed Breakfast Apple (p.214)

Lunch: Pumpkin and Pancetta Pasta (p.234). Piece of fruit

Dinner: Salad of Spinach, Feta, Mint and Pine Nuts (p.250). Roast Trout Fillets with Bacon and Green Beans (p.276)

Day 7

Breakfast: Cereal and Fruit Juice (p.222)

Lunch: Roast Chicken with Lemon and Tarragon (p.254). Low-fat New York Lemon Cheesecake with Raspberries (p.296)

Dinner: Lentil Soup with Spinach (p.245)

Week 6

Day 1
Breakfast: Morning Super-nutrient Energizer Porridge (p.213)
Lunch: Salad of Spinach, Feta, Mint and Pine Nuts (p.250). Four dried
  apricots. Four walnuts
Dinner: French-style Chicken Soup (p.222). Omelette with Tomato and Fresh
  Basil (p.238). Low-fat New York Lemon Cheesecake with Raspberries
  (p.296)

Day 2
Breakfast: Cereal and Fruit Juice (p.222)
Lunch: Herby Cheese Field Mushrooms (p.232). Glass of milk
Dinner: Shepherd's Pie with Carb Curfew Crust (p.264). Small green salad
  with olive oil dressing

Day 3
Breakfast: Classic Porridge with Fruit, Yoghurt and Nuts (p.211)
Lunch: Country Vegetable Soup with Cheese Toast (p.228)
Dinner: Roast Trout Fillets with Bacon and Green Beans (p.276). Small green
  salad with olive oil dressing. Two cubes dark high-cocoa chocolate

Day 4
Breakfast: Savoury Scrambled Eggs (p.212)
Lunch: Chinese Chicken Noodle Salad with Toasted Almonds (p.240). Glass
  of milk
Dinner: Hotpot with Haricot or Cannellini Beans (p.291). Cinnamon-
  poached Fruit (p.302)

Day 5

Breakfast: Fibre Fueller Cereal (p.220)

Lunch: Salmon Pâté with Watercress Salad (p.252). One fresh orange

Dinner: Lamb Stew with Ginger and Mint, with Wilted Spinach Leaves (p.268). Mixed Berry Salad with Low-fat Creamy Dressing (p.298)

Day 6

Breakfast: Crunchy Pear and Yoghurt Energizer (p.223)

Lunch: Pumpkin and Pancetta Pasta (p.234). Small green salad

Dinner: Thai-style Steamed Hake with Spinach and Gingered Carrots (p.280). Cinnamon-poached Fruit (p.302)

Day 7

Breakfast: Savoury Cheese Toast (p.215)

Lunch: Roast Chicken with Lemon and Tarragon (p.254). Two cubes high-cocoa dark chocolate

Dinner: Minestrone Soup (p.282)

8 Meal Ideas and Recipes

Don't feel guilty about eating. Yes, feel guilty if you run over the neighbour's cat – but not about eating!

In this chapter you'll find some delicious GI-friendly recipes for your lunch and Carb Curfew dinners as well as lots of simpler meal ideas that you can pick and choose depending on your taste. There are plenty of breakfast ideas, too, for you to try. Each of the recipes is calorie counted and nutritionally analysed per serving.

Breakfasts

In my research for this book I found that people fell into three distinct camps when it came to breakfast: those who didn't eat breakfast; those who ate the same thing each morning; and those who loved variety, with different flavours and tastes. In this section you'll find a wide variety of breakfasts, tasty enough to tempt the most ardent non-breakfast eater! Remember, breakfast doesn't have to be eaten first thing in the morning – you may find it more satisfying to eat one of these breakfasts for elevenses, and it will stop you reaching for the biscuit tin.

Classic Porridge with Fruit, Yoghurt and Nuts

Serves 1

30g porridge oats made with water, topped with ½ small pot bio yoghurt, 2 chopped prunes and 4 chopped walnuts

½ grapefruit

Small glass of natural, no-added-sugar fruit juice

Calories:	349
Carbs:	59.92g
Protein:	10.95g
Fat:	11.36g
Saturated fat:	2.16g

Super-healthy Egg White Omelette

Serves 1

Omelette made with 2 egg whites and chopped spring onions and chives

1 slice mixed-grain bread topped with ½ mashed avocado

Small glass of orange juice

Calories:	265
Carbs:	34.1g
Protein:	11.54g
Fat:	6.29g
Saturated fat:	0.23g

Savoury Scrambled Eggs

Serves 1

2 eggs scrambled with 2 tablespoons sautéed green and red peppers and onions on
   a small whole-wheat pitta or 1 slice wholemeal toast

1 grilled tomato

Small glass of natural, no-added-sugar fruit juice

Calories:	340
Carbs:	36.05g
Protein:	10.92g
Fat:	6.60g
Saturated fat:	1.82g

Morning Super-nutrient Energizer Porridge

Serves 1

30g porridge oats made with water topped with 3 chopped almonds, ½ tablespoon
brown sugar or honey and 100ml skimmed or semi-skimmed milk
½ small cantaloupe melon filled with ½ pot bio natural yogurt

Calories:	309
Carbs:	51.26g
Protein:	14.69g
Fat:	7.52g
Saturated fat:	1.98g

Nutty-topped Muffin with Fruit Salad

Serves 1

Toasted wholemeal muffin or crumpet topped with ½ tablespoon natural cashew,
   almond or peanut butter
Small bowl fruit salad topped with ½ pot natural bio yoghurt or cottage cheese

Calories:	325
Carbs:	57.66g
Protein:	11.74g
Fat:	8.18g
Saturated fat:	1.73g

Baked Stuffed Breakfast Apple

This doubles up as an excellent dessert. To make breakfast really simple, bake this the night before and enjoy the following day.

Serves 1
1 medium cooking apple
½ teaspoon ground cinnamon
2 teaspoons brown sugar
2 tablespoons natural bio yoghurt

Wash and score the apple around its middle. Remove the core and sprinkle the cinnamon and sugar inside. Bake at 180°C/350°F/Gas Mark 4 for about an hour until soft. Top with the yoghurt when ready to serve.

Calories:	156
Carbs:	33.94g
Protein:	4.9g
Fat:	2.21g
Saturated fat:	1.08g

Savoury Cheese Toast

Walnut bread is available from good bakers and supermarkets. It's delicious thinly sliced then toasted.

Serves 1

2 thin slices walnut toast topped with thin slice of any hard cheese and sliced tomato, and grilled

Small glass of orange juice

Calories:	289
Carbs:	43.55g
Protein:	16.99g
Fat:	5.79g
Saturated fat:	2.68g

Fruity Wholemeal Toast

Fruit bread is available from good bakers and supermarkets.

Serves 1

2 slices fruit toast spread with low-fat cream cheese and topped with 3 chopped
    semi-dried apricots, figs or prunes
Small glass of natural, no-added-sugar fruit juice

Calories:	370
Carbs:	55.82g
Protein:	11.70g
Fat:	4.67g
Saturated fat:	0.57g

Fruity Toasted Teacake

Serves 1

Toasted wholemeal fruit teacake spread with ½ mashed banana and 2 chopped apricots

Small glass semi-skimmed or skimmed milk

Calories:	316
Carbs:	58.36g
Protein:	11.49g
Fat:	5.87g
Saturated fat:	1.58g

Banana Cherry Bread

This is delicious toasted for brunch, but also good in the afternoon when you know that you'll be cutting the carbs from your evening meal but need something to keep you going. Once it has cooled, you can freeze it in slices, slipping a piece of greaseproof paper between the slices. In the morning you need only remove a slice when you get up, leave it to defrost while you get dressed, and it'll be ready for toasting when you come down for breakfast.

Serves 6–8
Preparation time: 10 minutes
Cooking time: 1 hour
225g plain flour
1 teaspoon salt
1 heaped teaspoon baking powder
1 teaspoon ground cinnamon
110g caster sugar
1 egg, beaten
90g unsalted butter, melted
Few drops vanilla essence
3 very ripe bananas, mashed
90g dried sour cherries

Preheat the oven to 180°C/350°F/Gas Mark 4. Before you begin, grease the baking tin with a little baking spray, then coat it in a layer of flour to stop the bread sticking to the sides. Sift together the flour, salt, baking powder and cinnamon. Stir in the sugar. With a fork, mix in the egg, melted butter and vanilla essence. Add the mashed bananas and cherries and mix with the fork just until all the ingredients are incorporated: don't over-mix.

Spoon the mixture into the prepared tin and bake for 50–60 minutes until the loaf springs back when prodded. Leave in the tin for 10 minutes before turning out to cool.

Calories:	282
Carbs:	45.18g
Protein:	3.67g
Fat:	10.32g
Saturated fat:	8g

Fibre Fueller Cereal

For the puffed rice you can use Rice Crispies or try a variety from a health-food store.

Serves 2

1 tablespoon All Bran

1 tablespoon Shreddies or Shredded Wheat, crumbled

1 tablespoon puffed rice

1 dessertspoon wheat germ

2 pieces of any dried fruit, chopped

½ tablespoon chopped almonds

2 teaspoons ground flaxseeds

1 dessertspoon lecithin

Mix all the ingredients together. Pour over skimmed or semi-skimmed milk and top with 2 tablespoons natural bio yoghurt. Enjoy with a small glass of pineapple juice.

Calories:	169
Carbs:	30.45g
Protein:	4.70g
Fat:	4.71g
Saturated fat:	0.43g

Boiled Egg and Soldiers

Serves 1

Boiled egg with 1 slice wholemeal toast

1 glass tomato juice

¼ melon or pineapple

Calories:	232
Carbs:	32.59g
Protein:	12.58g
Fat:	6.80g
Saturated fat:	1.98g

Cereal and Fruit Juice

Serves 1

Small bowl of any bran-based cereal with no added sugar or salt, with skimmed or
    semi-skimmed milk, topped with ½ small banana

Small glass of natural, no-added-sugar fruit juice

Calories:	282
Carbs:	67.85g
Protein:	10.60g
Fat:	1.66g
Saturated fat:	0.52g

Crunchy Pear and Yoghurt Energizer

Serves 1

Small pot natural bio yoghurt with 1 chopped pear and 2 tablespoons All Bran cereal
   topped with skimmed milk and freshly grated nutmeg

Calories:	310
Carbs:	54.76g
Protein:	13.43g
Fat:	3.98g
Saturated fat:	1.92g

Healthy Cooked Breakfast

Serves 1

1 poached egg with 2 rashers lean grilled bacon and grilled tomato with 1 slice
    wholemeal toast spread with thin scrap of butter

Small glass of natural, no-added-sugar fruit juice

Calories:	320
Carbs:	36.02g
Protein:	22.17g
Fat:	10.60g
Saturated fat:	1.82g

Lunches

These lunches are light yet satisfying. The recipes are all GI-balanced, leaving you feeling alert and ready for the afternoon. Some are simple enough to rustle up in five minutes. Others are simple to prepare but smart enough to share with friends when entertaining. You'll find that some of them are also suitable as Carb Curfew suppers.

Cottage Cheese, Peach and Walnut Salad

This light summer lunch can be rustled up quickly. I actually enjoy it all year round, replacing the fresh peaches with a few tinned slices in winter.

Serves 1
Large handful salad leaves
1 teaspoon olive oil
Squeeze fresh lemon juice
100g cottage cheese
1 peach, sliced
5 walnuts or almonds, chopped

Dress the salad leaves with the olive oil and lemon juice. Top with the cottage cheese, sliced peach and chopped nuts.

Calories:	274
Carbs:	21.89g
Protein:	16.51g
Fat:	14.81g
Saturated fat:	2.24g

Pear, Gorgonzola and Walnut Salad

This makes a tasty lunch or simple supper starter. It's smart enough for a mid-week lunch with friends, and easy enough to be easily assembled at the last minute. The dressing can be made in advance, and you can also prepare the pear – but no more than an hour before using or it tends to look a little tired.

Serves 1

1 teaspoon olive oil

½ teaspoon balsamic vinegar

½ teaspoon runny honey

Pinch sea salt

Large handful salad leaves

50g Gorgonzola or any other ripe blue-veined cheese, diced

1 small ripe pear, peeled and sliced

4 walnuts, chopped

Make the dressing by mixing the oil, balsamic vinegar, honey and seasoning in a small cup. Leave to one side until ready to serve the salad.

Place the salad leaves in a small bowl, add the dressing and top with the crumbled Gorgonzola, pear slices and chopped walnuts.

Calories:	376
Carbs:	24.17g
Protein:	26.91g
Fat:	13.35g
Saturated fat:	10.00g

Country Vegetable Soup with Cheese Toast

Soup and grilled cheese toast is a great winter comforter. Rich in calcium from the cheese and fibre from the vegetables, it's a perfect all-round lunch. If you love making your own soups you can also try some of the other soup recipes below.

Serves 1

300g pot fresh vegetable soup (any fresh, chilled, vegetable-based soup – look for fewer than 40 calories per 100ml on the label)

2 slices wholemeal bread

50g hard cheese, sliced

Dash of Tabasco

1 tomato, sliced

Freshly ground black pepper

Heat the soup according to the instructions on the label. Meanwhile, toast the bread, add the cheese slices and sprinkle with Tabasco. Top with the tomato slices, sprinkle with black pepper and grill until the cheese melts.

Enjoy with a small glass of orange juice.

Calories:	458
Carbs:	67.10g
Protein:	24.25g
Fat:	10.99g
Saturated fat:	3.31g

Nutty Chicken Pitta Pockets

This filling lunch tastes great and is also popular with older children.

Serves 2

For the filling

2 tablespoons sliced almonds

2 small (or 1 large) chicken breasts, grilled and sliced

4 semi-dried apricots, chopped

1 small celery stalk

½ pot natural bio yoghurt

½ tablespoon Dijon mustard

½ teaspoon lemon zest

½ teaspoon honey

1 large wholemeal pitta pocket

Handful of watercress

Preheat the oven to 150°C/300°F/Gas Mark 2. Place the almonds on a baking sheet and bake for 7–8 minutes or until roasted. Leave to one side to cool then mix with all the remaining filling ingredients in a bowl.

Meanwhile, toast the large pitta bread and cut in half, stuffing the chicken salad into each pitta half, together with the watercress.

Calories:	402
Carbs:	39.01g
Protein:	38.67g
Fat:	11.9g
Saturated fat:	2.51g

Chicken, Avocado, Walnut and Watercress Salad in Granary Bread

Here I use mashed avocado as a healthy alternative to mayonnaise, providing all the creaminess that mayonnaise-lovers adore, but with added vitamin C and other goodies. A recent report in New Scientist said that eating a handful of walnuts a day is highly beneficial – they add a nice crunch to this sandwich.

Serves 2

Preparation time: 5 minutes

1 ripe avocado

Juice of ½ a lemon

Freshly ground black pepper

4 slices of granary bread

1 cooked chicken breast, sliced

1 bag watercress, washed and torn up so the stalks aren't too long

About 12 walnut halves, toasted for 7–8 minutes in a low oven (see page 229)

Peel and mash the avocado in a small bowl, combining with the lemon juice immediately to prevent it discoloring. Add a generous grinding of black pepper then spread the bread with this mixture.

Layer the chicken slices, watercress and walnuts onto the bread, sandwich together and serve with some extra watercress on the side.

Calories:	343
Carbs:	30.60g
Protein:	22.20g
Fat:	16.55g
Saturated fat:	2.51g

Stuffed Pitta Bread with Falafel

Falafels are a rich source of protein and dietary fibre. Most supermarkets sell falafels now – you'll find them in the chilled section. You can also find them in more specialist delis or health-food shops.

Serves 1

1 large falafel patty (or 3 small ones), kept whole or chopped roughly

1 small carrot, grated

2 lettuce leaves, shredded

1 teaspoon mustard or low-calorie salad dressing

1 whole-wheat pitta pocket or 2 slices wholemeal bread, toasted

1 teaspoon roasted tahini butter

⅓ medium tomato, sliced

Warm the falafel through under the grill. Meanwhile, mix the grated carrot and shredded lettuce leaves with the dressing. Toast the pitta bread, spilt in half and spread with the tahini butter. Stuff with the warm falafel, the carrot and lettuce mixture and the tomato.

Calories:	351
Carbs:	49.04g
Protein:	13.46g
Fat:	12.83g
Saturated fat:	1.70g

Herby Cheese Field Mushrooms

I love this seasonal tasty dish. My Mum's best friend, Jean, introduced it to me after we'd been for a long walk in the country. Since then I've made many different versions, adding lean grilled bacon, replacing the herb cheese for cottage cheese and basically adapting it to whatever is in my house. Here I've kept it close to Jean's original — the mushrooms on that first occasion were freshly picked so it was totally delicious.

Serves 2

4 small slices wholemeal bread

4 large, flat field mushrooms, stalks removed

4 fresh basil leaves

1 teaspoon olive oil (truffle oil or any infused oil makes this extra special)

2 tablespoons reduced-fat herby cheese, such as Boursin

1 large tomato, sliced

Freshly ground black pepper

Handful salad leaves

With a large biscuit or scone cutter, cut four bread rounds and toast. Leave to one side.

Wash the field mushrooms, then place a large basil leaf on the dark side of each mushroom and drizzle with the olive oil. Pop under a hot grill for about 5 minutes until soft and the juices are starting to run, but make sure it does not burn. Remove from the grill and spread each mushroom with ½ tablespoon of the herby cheese. Place a tomato slice on top, sprinkle with black pepper and return to the hot grill until the cheese starts to melt and the tomato to brown.

Remove from the grill and place one mushroom on each toast round. Serve on a handful of salad leaves.

Calories:	234
Carbs:	34.37g
Protein:	11.32g
Fat:	7.40g
Saturated fat:	1.05g

Pumpkin and Pancetta Pasta

Roasted pumpkin is a real favourite of mine. There's something very comforting about its autumnal taste. Here I have combined it with some pancetta to make a tasty, substantial lunch. I generally use pumpkin left over from the night before, which I have roasted with a little olive oil, herbs and garlic cloves. Cold roasted pumpkin also works well tossed through a spinach leaf salad and topped with warm, lean, chopped bacon and a couple of slices of avocado. Try it.

Peperoncino is an Italian dried chilli, available from good delicatessens. If you can't find peperoncino, use a small pinch of dried chilli flakes, according to taste.

Serves 1
¼ pumpkin
Olive oil spray
Pinch dried thyme and oregano
2 cloves garlic, sliced finely
1 onion, chopped finely
50g pancetta (raw weight)
30g dried pasta, such as spaghetti or tagliatelle
1 tablespoon olive oil
Large handful fresh flat-leaf parsley, chopped finely
Pinch peperoncino, to taste

Preheat the oven to 200°C/400°F/Gas Mark 6. Spray the pumpkin quarter with olive oil, and sprinkle with thyme, oregano and a few slices of the garlic. Roast in the oven for about 45 minutes, or until the pumpkin is soft all the way through and golden brown. If necessary, take out every 15 minutes and respray with olive oil to prevent it drying out. When roasted, remove from the oven and set to one side.

While the pumpkin is roasting, dry sauté the onion and remaining garlic until soft. Add the pancetta, turning up the heat, and sauté until the pancetta is crispy.

Cook the pasta according to packet instructions. While the pasta is cooking, peel the pumpkin from its skin and cut into bite-size cubes. Drain the pasta when cooked, reserving a little of the water. Add the olive oil to the pasta, together with lots of black pepper, chopped flat-leaf parsley and peperoncino to taste. Stir well, adding a little of the reserved pasta water if it looks a little dry as the pumpkin will quickly soak up the juices. Add the pancetta, onion and cubed pumpkin, stir over a low heat to warm through and serve with a green salad.

Calories:	348
Carbs:	36.93g
Protein:	16.62g
Fat:	14.42g
Saturated fat:	2.96g

Crab Cakes with Crunchy Warm Coleslaw

This requires a little more time to make but is worth it, and looks great if you have friends round for lunch. Crab meat is particularly low in fat and a great source of protein, and the flavours work really well together.

Serves 4

Preparation time: 20 minutes

Cooking time: 10 minutes

225g crab meat

1 stick celery, chopped finely

½ tablespoon fat-free mayonnaise

½ tablespoon lemon juice

Freshly ground black pepper

Pinch curry powder

Pinch cayenne pepper, to taste

Pinch mustard powder

1 tablespoon chopped chives

½ tablespoon chopped fresh dill

1–3 drops Tabasco (optional), to taste

1 egg, beaten, to bind

1–2 tablespoons fresh wholemeal breadcrumbs

Handful of salad leaves

4 thin slices wholemeal bread, cut into rounds and toasted

Mix all the ingredients, except the bread rounds, in a large bowl, adding the beaten egg and breadcrumbs last so you get the consistency right. The crab cakes should be wet enough to stick together without being soggy. Using your hands, roll the mixture to form 4 large cakes. Heat a large non-stick pan and add the crab cakes, cooking for about 4–5 minutes on each side until brown. You shouldn't need any oil but if in doubt add a tablespoon of water to avoid sticking. Serve warm on a bed of salad leaves or on each of the toasted wholemeal rounds.

Calories:	171
Carbs:	18.58g
Protein:	15.21g
Fat:	3.78g
Saturated fat:	0.8g

Omelette with Tomato and Fresh Basil

Eggs are just about my favourite all-round simple food. Rich in choline – important for brain function – they are cheap, tasty and a permanent fixture in my fridge. I often poach a couple of eggs and have them soft over a green salad. This omelette is quickly put together, and the basil and tomato really bring the eggs alive without the need for lots of salt.

Serves 1

1 tomato

Salt and freshly ground black pepper

Handful of fresh basil leaves, torn

1 teaspoon olive oil

2 eggs

1 tablespoon skimmed milk

Chop the tomato and put in a bowl with the seasoning, basil and ½ teaspoon of the olive oil. Beat the eggs and milk together and season with black pepper. If you prefer a fluffier omelette, separate the egg whites first and whisk until they form soft peaks, season and gently fold in the egg yolks.

Heat the remaining oil in a small, non-stick pan until the pan is hot. Pour the egg mixture into the pan, cooking slowly so the egg starts to set throughout.

Everyone has their own preferred way of cooking an omelette. Personally, I like my omelettes soft, so as I move the eggs around I add the tomato mixture just as the eggs look as if they are starting to set. Continue to cook through to your desired consistency, fold and turn out on to a warm plate.

Calories:	249
Carbs:	9.13g
Protein:	17.22g
Fat:	15.01g
Saturated fat:	4.11g

Chinese Chicken Noodle Salad with Toasted Almonds

Dan, my partner, loves his noodles, and I can put this together for us pretty quickly. The red cabbage is rich in phytonutrients and the almonds are a good source of essential fats. For speed, I often use up leftover chicken from the night before or chunks from the Roast Chicken with Lemon and Tarragon Sunday roast (see page 256).

Serves 4

Preparation time: 12 minutes

Small cos lettuce, torn into bite-size pieces

¼ head red cabbage

4 spring onions

25g Chinese chow mein noodles, steamed, drained and left in a little of the cooking water to prevent sticking

4 small or 3 large chicken breasts, grilled and sliced

25g chopped roasted almonds

For the dressing

2 tablespoons vegetable oil

2 tablespoons rice vinegar

1 tablespoon reduced-sodium soy sauce

½ tablespoon sesame oil

1 tablespoon sugar

2 tablespoons vegetable stock

Make the dressing by mixing together all the ingredients in a small bowl.

In a large bowl, combine the lettuce, cabbage, spring onions, noodles and dressing. Top with the sliced chicken and toasted almonds.

Calories:	351
Carbs:	21.02g
Protein:	25.11g
Fat:	19.07g
Saturated fat:	2.19g

Healthy Eggs Benedict

You can't beat eggs Benedict, but it can often be a bit hefty in saturated fat and calories. This healthy version is much lighter but still tasty. Enjoy it with a glass of fresh orange juice and you'll help your body absorb the iron from the spinach. Frozen chopped spinach is a great vegetable to have in your freezer. It cooks really quickly and can be added to any casserole dish or can make a simple, healthy vegetable accompaniment.

Serves 1
50g spinach
2 slices lean bacon
1 large tomato, halved
½ tablespoon fat-free mayonnaise
1 tablespoon low-fat natural bio yoghurt
Tabasco sauce, to taste (optional)
2 eggs
1 small wholemeal muffin

Steam the spinach until tender, drain and leave to one side in the sieve to ensure any excess water is drained.

Grill the bacon and tomato; and mix together the mayo and natural yoghurt, adding the Tabasco if you prefer a bit of a kick.

Poach the eggs. Meanwhile, split the muffin and put in the toaster. Spread each half of the toasted muffin with a little of the yoghurt and mayo mixture, top with a slice of bacon and a poached egg, and spoon the remaining yoghurt and mayo mixture on top. Serve with the grilled tomato.

Calories:	400
Carbs:	39.42g
Protein:	22.89g
Fat:	17.78g
Saturated fat:	4.66g

Peanut Butter Sandwich with Crunchy Dipping Vegetables

If peanut butter is a new flavour to you, or something that tends to be in the house for the younger members of the family, then be bold and try this sandwich. Adding the wheat germ boosts the vitamin E content of this power-packed lunch, and honey is a good mood-booster as well as a nutrient-rich alternative to sugar or sugar substitutes.

For one round of sandwiches
2 slices medium-sliced wholemeal bread
1 tablespoon peanut butter (no added sugar or salt)
1 teaspoon honey
2 teaspoons wheat germ (blended with the honey)

For the crudités
1 small red bell pepper, sliced
3 tablespoons reduced-fat hummus

Make up the sandwich, spreading the peanut butter on 1 slice of bread and the honey and wheat germ mixture on the other. Sandwich them together and serve with the sliced red pepper and hummus, and a glass of skimmed milk.

Calories:	440
Carbs:	55.02g
Protein:	20.29g
Fat:	17.71g
Saturated fat:	3.44g

Lentil Soup with Spinach

Pulses are rich in protein and dietary fibre. Adding the spinach boosts the nutrient content of this lunch as well as making it more substantial. The bio yoghurt is a cooling natural alternative to cream and contrasts well with the textures of the spinach and the lentils. Drink a small glass of orange juice with your soup as the vitamin C will help your body absorb the iron in the spinach.

Serves 1

50g frozen chopped spinach

300g lentil soup (fresh from chill cabinet in any good supermarket)

1 tablespoon natural bio yoghurt

Fresh nutmeg, to garnish

1 small wholemeal roll

2 slices pineapple

Cook the chopped spinach and warm the soup through. Pour the soup into a bowl, top with the chopped spinach, and garnish with the natural yoghurt and a grating of fresh nutmeg. Serve with a small bread roll, and cleanse your palate with the pineapple.

Calories:	357
Carbs:	69.11g
Protein:	15.48g
Fat:	4.01g
Saturated fat:	0.75g

Chicken Liver Pâté

Made ahead, chicken liver pâté is a simple, easy lunch, and offal is believed to be particularly beneficial for arthritis sufferers. You can also enjoy it as a starter for a more formal supper.

This pâté goes beautifully with Melba toast or any thin cracker, Cumberland sauce or fruit jelly, and a good peppery salad like watercress or rocket on the side.

This recipe makes enough for four servings – it's not worth making smaller quantities and the pâté keeps in the fridge for a week. For the pots that you're not going to use immediately it's important to pour on a little melted butter to prevent the pâté from oxidizing and turning grey: you can scrape off the butter before eating to avoid extra calories.

Serves 4
Preparation time: 10 minutes
Cooking time: 20 minutes (plus chilling time)
¼ lb chicken livers
1 shallot, sliced finely
55g butter
1 clove garlic, sliced finely
Salt and pepper
1 teaspoon brandy

Wash the chicken livers, trimming off any membrane.

Sauté the sliced shallot in half of the butter until soft and golden. Add the garlic, livers, a grinding of pepper and a tiny pinch of salt. Cook gently until the livers are brown on the outside but retain some pinkness inside. When they are done, add the remaining butter and the brandy and remove from the heat.

Allow the pâté to cool for 10 minutes, then either liquidize it or press through a sieve with a wooden spoon to get rid of lumps. Pour into small pots or ramekin dishes and chill so that it sets before serving.

To make Melba toast, preheat the oven to 180°C/350°F/Gas Mark 4. Lightly toast some medium slices of white bread on one side under the grill. Leave to cool for a minute or so then cut into triangles (removing the crusts if you want to). You want the slices to be extra thin, so lay the bread flat on the work surface and use the palm of your hand to keep the toast flat while you slice *carefully* through with a bread knife. Place the triangles, toasted side down, on a baking tray and bake for about 5 minutes until golden brown. Remove and cool on a rack. You'll need to watch them like a hawk as they burn easily.

For the pâté only	
Calories:	75
Carbs:	1.32g
Protein:	5.69g
Fat:	4.09g
Saturated fat:	2.20g

Chicken and Spinach Salad

Quick, colourful and tasty, this is a great salad all year round, especially since freshly packed spinach is so widely available. Opting for walnut bread as opposed to regular wholemeal will give you an extra boost of essential fatty acids as well as being good for your brain power.

Serves 1
75g baby spinach leaves, washed
1 medium tomato, chopped
2 tablespoons chopped red onion
1 large carrot, grated
2 tablespoons vinaigrette dressing made with safflower oil
75g roasted chicken breast, sliced
1 slice walnut bread

Arrange the spinach leaves, tomato, carrot and red onion in a salad bowl. Toss with the vinaigrette and top with the sliced roasted chicken breast. Serve with the walnut bread.

Calories:	355
Carbs:	32.54g
Protein:	32.96g
Fat:	10.58g
Saturated fat:	1.18g

Melon and Parma Ham with Mint Vinaigrette

This 1970s' starter is still good, but it can also be revived as a light, refreshing lunch. Make sure that the melons are perfectly ripe – you can ascertain this simply by smelling them. To make it more visually exciting, use two types of melon – one green-fleshed such as Ogen, the other orange-fleshed such as Charentais – and save leftovers for dessert or lunch the next day. They keep well in the fridge when cut if wrapped in clingfilm.

Serves 2
Preparation time: 10 minutes
Bag of baby salad leaves
Handful mint leaves, torn
1 medium or 2 small melons
4 slices Parma ham
2 tablespoons olive oil
½ tablespoon cider vinegar

Mix the salad leaves with ¾ of the torn mint, and lay out on each plate. Scoop the melon flesh with a melon baller, slice thinly or cut into cubes. Cut the Parma ham into strips. Arrange them all prettily on the salad leaves.

In a small bowl, mix the oil and vinegar together with a fork or small whisk, and then drizzle it over the melon and ham. Garnish with more torn mint leaves.

Calories:	306
Carbs:	29.99g
Protein:	12.74g
Fat:	17.10g
Saturated fat:	3.07g

Salad of Spinach, Feta, Mint and Pine Nuts

This can be a light lunch with a few crispbreads (try Dr Karg's organic seeded crispbreads) or a vegetarian sandwich filling, with the mint leaves giving bursts of fresh flavour.

You can buy feta pre-wrapped and preserved in water, but some deli counters now keep it in bowls covered with olive oil – try to find this if you can, as the cheese will have absorbed some of the flavour of the olive oil. Adding rocket to the spinach gives a peppery kick.

Serves 2

Preparation time: 10 minutes

Cooking time: 5 minutes

30g pine nuts

2 tablespoons extra virgin olive oil

1–2 teaspoons white wine vinegar

100g feta cheese, crumbled (with any oil it comes in)

Handful (15g) mint leaves, roughly torn

1 bag baby spinach leaves (or half spinach, half rocket)

Toast the pine nuts to bring out their flavour: heat them over a medium flame in a heavy-based saucepan, stirring constantly to stop them sticking. When they begin to take on a bit of colour, pour them on to a cold plate and leave them to cool.

Mix the olive oil and vinegar, then toss with the cooled pine nuts and all the other ingredients. Serve.

Calories:	285
Carbs:	3.46g
Protein:	9.96g
Fat:	25.93g
Saturated fat:	9.64g

Salmon Pâté with Watercress Salad

This takes only five minutes to make, so keep the ingredients to hand in case you need an impromptu lunch dish or starter for dinner. The key is fresh tarragon, chives and lemon zest: chives grow quite happily in sheltered pots providing you snip them regularly, and French tarragon grows well against a protected wall (Russian tarragon grows better, but doesn't taste nearly as good). Salmon and watercress is a classic combination, but do vary the leaves to see which you prefer.

It's difficult to be precise about the yoghurt quantities as different brands vary in terms of how set they are. Start out with one spoonful, mix well, and then add more until you begin to taste the yoghurt, but before it gets too sloppy.

Serves 8
Preparation time: 5 minutes

For the salmon pâté
1 tin (418g) red salmon
50g low-fat mayonnaise
15g fresh tarragon, leaves only, chopped
15g fresh chives, chopped
Zest of 1 lemon, chopped finely
50–100g low-fat natural yoghurt

For the watercress salad
4 packs watercress (or any green salad leaf except iceberg lettuce)
4 tablespoons olive oil
2 tablespoons tarragon vinegar (or white wine vinegar and a few chopped tarragon
   leaves)
Freshly ground black pepper

Drain the salmon well, and then pick it over and remove any large bones, vertebrae and skin. Put into a mixing bowl and stir in the mayonnaise, tarragon, chives and lemon zest. Add 1 tablespoon of yoghurt, and stir well with a fork until creamy: if you use a hand mixer you'll lose texture but gain creaminess – the choice is up to you. Add more yoghurt until you get the right taste. If you feel you need more lemon, then use the zest of another lemon rather than the juice, which will thin out the pâté.

Pile into individual ramekins or one large bowl, decorate with watercress leaves, lemon zest or anything else that takes your fancy, cover with clingfilm and place in the fridge. If you leave it in the fridge for a while the herbs will lose some of their potency, so sprinkle more over the top just before you serve it.

When you are ready to serve, mix the oil and vinegar together and toss the salad with the dressing. Serve either with good granary bread or crispbreads.

Calories:	165
Carbs:	1.96g
Protein:	12.11g
Fat:	12.19g
Saturated fat:	2.15g

Roast Chicken with Lemon and Tarragon

Roast chicken is the perfect Sunday lunch. Children love it with roast potatoes. Sweet potatoes, a lower-calorie alternative, are used here as well; they
bake to a delicious caramelized purée and are delicious with the lemony tar-
ragony gravy. Team it all with stir-fried green cabbage.

Serves 4

The chicken
1 chicken weighing around 1.5 kg, preferably free-range
1 bunch tarragon
1 dessertspoon (30g) butter
1 organic lemon, sliced in half

The sweet potatoes
Allow 1 per person

The roast potatoes
Allow 2 medium-sized potatoes per person

The cabbage
5 handfuls shredded green cabbage
2–3 rashers streaky bacon
1 teaspoon olive oil

Preheat the oven to 230°C/450°F/Gas Mark 8. Wash and dry the chicken.
   Chop the tarragon, removing the stalks, and mix with the softened butter.
Gently ease back the skin on the breast and rub in the herby butter. Place the
lemon halves in the cavity of the chicken, put it in a snug-fitting roasting tin

and place in the oven. After 15 minutes, baste the chicken and lower the heat to 190°C/375°F/Gas Mark 5. It will be ready in an hour.

While the chicken is cooking, wash and dry the sweet potatoes, cut them into large chunks and place on a baking tray in the oven. Peel the other potatoes, chop them into chunks the same size as the sweet potatoes and bring to the boil in a saucepan. Heat some sunflower oil in another roasting tin, drain the potatoes when they come to the boil, toss in the oil and place in the oven.

Wash and dry the cabbage leaves, then shred them. Cut up the rashers of bacon and cook gently in a pan in the olive oil until the fat melts. Remove from the heat and set aside.

When the chicken has been at the lower heat for an hour, check it by sticking a knife into the thigh. If the juices run clear it is ready. Remove it from the oven. Lift the chicken on to a serving dish and cover with foil. It can rest for 10 minutes, while you prepare the cabbage and gravy.

Put the frying pan or wok with the bacon back on the heat, add the cabbage and stir-fry until done, adding a little water if necessary. For the gravy, add a glass of white wine to the roasting pan juices and allow to bubble, skimming the fat off the top.

Put the sweet potatoes directly on to a serving dish, and drain the roast potatoes on some kitchen roll.

Serve and enjoy.

Calories:	431
Carbs:	67.61g
Protein:	17.89g
Fat:	11.32g
Saturated fat:	2.93g

Carb Curfew Dinners

I really hope you enjoy my Carb Curfew suppers – they are delicious enough to convert even the most ardent starchy-carb fanatic. Again, all the recipes are GI-friendly as well as jam-packed with goodness. There are vegetarian options, as well as vegetarian suggestions in some of the meat recipes. You'll find recipes suitable for entertaining as well as for simple midweek suppers – and some ideas for younger family members.

Meat Dishes

Braised Chicken and Fennel with Leeks and Green Beans

Poaching is a great low-fat way to cook chicken, and also ensures that it does not dry out, which can be a real problem with chicken breasts. You can use any part of the chicken for this – if you leave the bone in you get more flavour, but it takes a little longer to cook. It is worth seeking out fennel seeds for this dish as they give a real depth of flavour.

If you would prefer a vegetarian option, then substitute vegetable stock for the chicken stock and use one can (410g weight) of butterbeans or chickpeas in place of the chicken, just heating the beans through in the stock.

Serves 2
Preparation time: 10 minutes
Cooking time: 30 minutes
200g skinless chicken (boned weight) or 250g with bones in: any cut you like
250ml good chicken stock

Zest and juice of 1 lemon

1 teaspoon fennel seeds

1 teaspoon olive oil

1 medium onion, sliced

2 medium leeks, washed and sliced

2 medium bulbs fennel, cored and thinly sliced (reserve green fronds for decoration)

200g French beans, topped, tailed and chopped in half

2 cloves garlic, finely chopped

Cut any remaining fat off the chicken and either leave the size it is or cut into bite-size chunks. Bring the chicken stock to a gentle simmer, add the chicken, a strip of lemon zest and the fennel seeds to it and poach it gently, uncovered, for 10 minutes or until it is done (check to make sure that it doesn't dry out: if it looks like sticking, add more chicken stock or water). Set aside off the heat while you deal with the vegetables.

Heat the oil in a largish frying pan, and sauté the onion slices until soft. Add the leeks and fry until they too are softening and beginning to brown. Add the fennel slices, beans and chopped garlic and fry until the fennel begins to soften but the beans retain some crunch. Squeeze half the lemon over it, mix well, taste, and lay on plates before pouring the braised chicken and its juices over the top.

Chop the fennel fronds and remaining lemon zest together and sprinkle over the top.

Calories:	296
Carbs:	22.48g
Protein:	35.21g
Fat:	7.77g
Saturated fat:	1.58g

Estela's One Pan Easy Supper

This is fast, easy and made in just one pan. My mother-in-law, Estela, devised this recipe at her home in Venice, which has very limited cooking space. When we get invited round for supper we have only one pan to wash up afterwards – so we are all happy!

Serves 4

3 chicken breasts, thinly sliced horizontally into 6 pieces in total

Juice and zest of 1 lemon

2 tablespoons olive oil

Coarse black pepper

Pinch peperoncino flakes (optional), to taste

6 shallots, sliced

5–6 cloves garlic, sliced thinly

1 red bell pepper, sliced

400g tin chopped tomatoes

Large handful chopped parsley

Salt and black pepper to taste

Marinate the chicken breast slices in the lemon juice and zest, olive oil, coarse black pepper and peperoncino flakes for at least 2 hours – longer is better. I often put them in to marinate first thing in the morning.

When you are ready to eat, brown the chicken breast slices in a large preheated pan. Do not add any more oil. Take out of the pan and leave to one side. In the same pan, add the shallots, garlic, red pepper, tomatoes and lots of chopped parsley. Add a little more black pepper, a pinch of salt and, if you want, a little more peperoncino. My partner's family are from Argentina so they like it with a bit of a kick – but it took me quite a while to get the correct amount! Stir and bring to a gentle simmer and leave for about 30 minutes, then add the chicken and cook through to heat.

> **Tip:** It's really easy to make a little more sauce – just double the sauce ingredients. You can then use this as a sauce to enjoy with tagliatelle pasta the following day for lunch.

Calories:	214
Carbs:	11.81g
Protein:	21.62g
Fat:	9.32g
Saturated fat:	1.59g

Salad of Turkey Breast with Lentils, Mushrooms and Watercress

This delicious recipe is easy to prepare and full of fibre and vitamins. It's a good idea to keep cans of lentils in the store cupboard, and good stock (vegetable, beef or chicken) in the freezer – if all else fails you can simply heat the lentils through with the stock, add seasoning and herbs to taste, and swirl in a little low-fat yoghurt for an instant soup.

Serves 2

Preparation time: 10 minutes

Cooking time: 15 minutes

570ml stock (chicken or vegetable)

1 turkey breast

200g mushrooms

2 tablespoons olive oil

1 tin Puy lentils

Salt and freshly ground black pepper

1 bag watercress, stalks cut into small lengths

Juice of ½ a lemon

Bring the stock to the boil, add the turkey breast and simmer gently for 10–12 minutes. Allow to cool in the poaching liquid.

Slice the mushrooms, heat half of the olive oil and turn the mushroom slices in it. Add a tablespoon of the poaching liquid and cover. Cook over a gentle heat, shaking occasionally, for 5 minutes. While this is cooking, drain the lentils and stir into the mushrooms with more poaching liquid if required. Season to taste.

Make a dressing for the watercress with the remaining olive oil, the lemon juice and lots of black pepper. Slice the turkey breast and serve on a bed of the lentil and mushroom mixture, with the dressed watercress on the side.

Calories:	348
Carbs:	26.42g
Protein:	29.42g
Fat:	14.97g
Saturated fat:	2.14g

Grilled Pork Steaks with Spicy Sweetcorn Salsa

This very simple dish is great for a quick supper, and full of colour and flavour. You will have more sweetcorn than you need, so either whiz any leftovers with some vegetable or chicken stock to make a soup, or toss it into some rocket leaves and pile into pitta bread for lunch the next day. The sweetcorn salsa benefits from being made up to a day in advance, so it is easy to serve this for a dinner party, adding a green salad dressed with pumpkin seeds, olive oil and lemon juice on the side. The colours will really lift your spirits!

Serves 2, with leftover sweetcorn

Preparation time: 20 minutes (plus time to marinate)

Cooking time: 10 minutes

2 pork steaks (150g each), fat removed

1 juicy lime

1 teaspoon hot paprika (or ½ teaspoon sweet paprika mixed
    with ½ teaspoon chilli powder)

1 teaspoon olive oil

1 clove garlic, peeled and diced finely

1 large carrot, peeled and diced finely

1 tin (350g) sugar-free sweetcorn

½ chicken or vegetable stock cube

50g fresh coriander, rinsed, dried and finely chopped

2 spring onions, including green bits, finely chopped

As early as you can (in the morning, if you are organized), place the pork steaks on a plate and squeeze half the lime juice over them, turning them to coat. With the back of a spoon, spread a generous pinch of hot paprika (or a small pinch of sweet paprika and a small pinch of chilli powder) over each side of the meat. Cover with clingfilm and leave to marinate for as long as you can in the refrigerator. Remember to bring the meat back to room temperature before you cook it.

To prepare the salsa, heat the olive oil in a heavy-based pan over a medium flame. Add the diced garlic and carrot and fry gently until the carrot begins to soften. Add the tinned sweetcorn, including any water in the tin, the remaining hot paprika or paprika/chilli mix, and crumble the half stock cube into the pan. Stir to mix well, and then simmer gently with the lid on for 10 minutes. Check that the salsa doesn't dry out – if it is beginning to stick then add a splash of water. You can stop at this stage if you are preparing it in advance.

When you are ready to cook, preheat the grill to high. Place the pork steaks, with their marinade, under the grill and cook for 5 minutes on each side until cooked all the way through. As they are cooking, reheat the sweetcorn salsa gently, stirring in half the chopped coriander and half the chopped spring onions.

To serve, place a good spoonful of the salsa on a plate and lay the grilled pork on top. Mix the remaining spring onions and coriander together, and sprinkle over the whole dish.

Calories:	373
Carbs:	38.96g
Protein:	34.03g
Fat:	11.03g
Saturated fat:	2.83g

Shepherd's Pie with Carb Curfew Crust

Shepherd's pie is such a traditional dish that it's difficult to tamper with. The mashed potato topping is very heavy on the carbs, however, so here is a nifty way of making a Carb Curfew crust. Others may find it difficult to forego their mashed potato topping, but this is easily remedied by making two pies. If you have cold roast lamb then by all means use it: otherwise use fresh lamb mince. The gentle simmering process is essential – if you turn up the heat to shorten the cooking time you'll end up with rubber. The meat mixture freezes very well, so make plenty in advance and have it on hand for quick suppers.

Serves 4
Preparation time: 45 minutes
Cooking time: 30 minutes
1 teaspoon vegetable oil
2 medium onions, chopped
2 sticks celery, chopped
2 medium carrots, chopped
400g minced lamb, or minced roast lamb
1 glass red wine (optional)
500ml vegetable, chicken or lamb stock
2 bay leaves
1 teaspoon fresh thyme leaves
1–2 teaspoons Worcestershire sauce
200g mashing potatoes
1 tablespoon butter
2 tablespoons milk
5–6 leaves filo pastry

Preheat the oven to 200°C/400°F/Gas Mark 6. In a heavy casserole dish, heat the oil and fry the onions, celery and carrots until soft and beginning to brown. Add the lamb mince and fry till it loses its pink colour, then add the wine, if using, and cook until all the liquid bubbles away. Add the stock, bay and thyme leaves and simmer gently for about 35 minutes until the mixture has thickened. Add a teaspoon of Worcestershire sauce, taste and correct the seasoning. If you are planning to freeze the mixture, this is the place to stop: defrost it completely and remember to bring the mix up to room temperature before you cook it.

When you are ready to cook the pies, divide the meat mixture between two dishes. Cook and mash the potatoes as usual, adding the butter and milk to lighten them. Pile the mashed potatoes on to the non-Carb Curfew pie, and flatten and decorate the top with the tines of a fork.

On the Carb Curfew pie, gently scrunch up the leaves of filo pastry and arrange them on the surface (you may need more sheets, depending on the shape of your pie dish). Place the pies in the oven and cook for about 25 minutes until the toppings are brown and the mixture bubbling. The filo may cook more quickly than the potato, so have a sheet of baking parchment or grease-proof paper on hand to place over the top if it begins to burn.

Serve with more Worcestershire sauce and some lovely green peas.

Carb Curfew version:	
Calories:	442
Carbs:	47.42g
Protein:	32.35g
Fat:	22.04g
Saturated fat:	8.56g

Lamb Chops with Mixed Peppercorns

This quick and easy supper can be made really special by picking good meat and removing it from the fridge at least half an hour before cooking. This recipe takes no time at all, so get organized first – warm your plates and set the table.

Serves 2

Preparation time: 5 minutes

Cooking time: 10 minutes

2 lamb chops of your choice, preferably evenly cut and quite thick

1 teaspoon olive oil

1 teaspoon mixed peppercorns, cracked (a mortar and pestle is good for this)

1 tin Puy lentils

1 shallot, finely sliced

2 large handfuls green beans, French or runner

For the gravy (optional)

1 glass of wine, ½ glass of stock

Heat a very heavy frying pan over a medium heat until the pan shimmers. Smear the olive oil on to the chops, and press the cracked peppercorns firmly into both sides.

Pour the lentils into a saucepan, add the finely sliced shallot, stir and leave on a low heat to warm through. Boil some salted water for the beans.

Lay the chops in the hot pan and cook for 3–4 minutes. Turn them with a spatula and cook for another 2–3 minutes. To test for doneness, give the meat a little prod – if you want it rare, remove when the meat still feels soft; for medium, remove when it still has a little give; and for well-done, leave until the meat feels hard. When done to your taste, remove the meat from the pan and leave it to rest for a couple of minutes on a plate in a warm place. This gives you time to make gravy and to pop the beans into the water to cook.

If you are making gravy, return the pan to the heat and deglaze with a glass of wine. Reduce by about half, then add the stock and any juices which may have accumulated under the chops. Drain the beans and arrange on warmed plates with the lentils and chops. Serve with the gravy if desired.

Calories:	403
Carbs:	25.39g
Protein:	35.93g
Fat:	17.65g
Saturated fat:	6.93g

Lamb Stew with Ginger and Mint, with Wilted Spinach Leaves

A gentle curry for cold evenings, this is inspired by a recipe in the American food magazine *Bon Appetit*. It's made easy by the availability of puréed ginger and garlic (look for the Barts brand in the supermarket), which keep in the fridge for weeks. They're also essential ingredients for stir-fries, so it's well worth investing in a small jar of each.

Cutting the lamb into small pieces means you can still use a stewing type of meat rather than the more expensive steaks – but if you feel like pushing the boat out then by all means go for the richer cuts. Garam masala is a mixed curry spice that you can find in the herb sections in supermarkets. The red lentils add both fibre and protein – they're also a useful store cupboard food as you can throw a handful into soups and stews to give a bit of body as they cook down into a creamy sauce.

For a vegetarian version of this, substitute a can (410g) of chickpeas for the lamb.

Serves 2

Preparation time: 20 minutes

Cooking time: 30 minutes max

2 tablespoons vegetable oil (groundnut oil works well here)

2 medium onions, thinly sliced

250g lamb neck fillet, cut into ½-inch cubes

1 teaspoon puréed garlic

2 teaspoons puréed ginger

2 teaspoons garam masala

¼–½ red chilli, chopped finely (optional)

15g fresh coriander, chopped finely

15g fresh mint, chopped finely

100g red lentils

20g raisins (optional)

1 bag baby spinach leaves, washed and dried

Heat the vegetable oil in a heavy-based pan and fry the onions until beginning to brown. Remove to a plate and set aside. In the same pan, fry the lamb cubes until brown all over, then add the garlic, ginger, garam masala, chilli (if using), half the fresh coriander and half the fresh mint. Stir until the wonderful aromas are released.

Add 250ml water and the lentils, put the lid on tightly and simmer slowly for 15 minutes until the lentils are beginning to break down and the lamb is done (this timing will depend on the size of the lamb pieces, but 15–20 minutes should be sufficient). If you like a sweet-and-sour flavour to your curries, add the raisins now. Check after 10 minutes to see if you need to add any more water to stop the lentils sticking and to keep its stew-like texture.

When the lamb is tender, stir in the cooked onion mixture and warm through. Check for seasoning and texture (you may need to add a little more water). Put the raw spinach leaves on warm plates, and then pile the stew on top of them – the heat of the stew will cook the spinach for you. Garnish with the remaining fresh coriander and fresh mint.

Calories:	458
Carbs:	21.29g
Protein:	37.08g
Fat:	19.83g
Saturated fat:	8.09g

Stir-fried Beef with Grilled Asparagus and a Lemon and Thyme Dressing

This light supper dish is quick to prepare and lovely to look at. You can easily double or triple the quantities if you want to serve it for more people. The thinner you slice the beef the better – either get a butcher to do it for you, or make sure that you have a very sharp knife to hand.

Serves 2

Preparation time: 10 minutes

Cooking time: 10 minutes

1 dessertspoonful fresh thyme leaves, destalked as much as possible

Pinch of salt

A few grindings of pepper

1 tablespoon lemon juice

4 tablespoons olive oil

1 bunch asparagus (about 200g), as fresh as possible

250g beef, chuck or rump, sliced into strips against the grain

Wash and dry the thyme leaves, add salt and pepper, and either chop finely with a very sharp knife or grind with a mortar and pestle. Add the lemon juice and stir well to mix. Then stir in 3 tablespoons of the oil. Set aside.

Prepare the asparagus by breaking off the ends of the stalks at the weakest point, and peeling the stalks with a potato peeler if they look tough. Place in a single layer on a grill pan and brush with olive oil. Set the grill to medium, and grill, turning occasionally, for 5–10 minutes.

Heat a wok or large frying pan, then add the remaining tablespoon of oil. When it begins to smoke, add the strips of beef and cook, stirring constantly, for 2–3 minutes.

Serve with the asparagus, and the dressing spooned over both.

Calories:	407
Carbs:	3.89g
Protein:	30.23g
Fat:	30.30g
Saturated fat	4.76g

Grilled Steak with Roasted Beetroot and Creamed Spinach

This is a great dish to be eaten hot, but the leftover steak strips and beetroot are also sublime cold with a green salad. Steak is a luxury, but it is worth buying good meat that has been well-hung and has a lovely dark-red colour to it. You can use rump, fillet or sirloin for this dish – if you're feeding friends as well then it's nice to roast it whole for effect, but if you want to be more informal it may be easier to grill individual steaks. The beetroot takes 1–1½hours, but you're not doing anything to it in that time. It's important to use fresh beetroot for this, as roasting gives it a wonderfully intense flavour. The technique for this is taken from a delicious Thai beef salad recipe in *Sophie Grigson's Meat Course*.

Serves 4

Preparation time: 10 minutes

Cooking time: 1½ hours max

4–6 medium fresh beetroot, leaves trimmed to about 1cm from the root

1 tablespoon peppercorns (optional)

2–3 tablespoons olive oil

1 tablespoon fresh thyme leaves

2 tablespoons balsamic vinegar

Zest of 1 orange

450g good lean steak (rump, fillet, sirloin)

600g frozen spinach

1 tablespoon walnut oil

30g chopped walnuts

20 chives, snipped small

Preheat the oven to 180°C/350°F/Gas Mark 4. Wash the beetroot gently without breaking the skin, and wrap them in foil. Roast in the top of the oven for 1–1½ hours, depending on their size (fist-sized will take 1½ hours, smaller ones less time).

While the beetroot are cooking, crush the peppercorns, if using, with the blade of a large flat knife, or in a mortar and pestle. Mix 1 tablespoon of oil and the thyme leaves and brush this mixture over both sides of the steak. Set aside until you are ready to cook it.

When the beetroot are done (a skewer goes through them readily), unwrap and remove the skin using a sharp paring knife and fork. Slice them, and put into an ovenproof dish. Stir over the balsamic vinegar, remaining oil and half the orange zest, check the taste (you may want to add a squeeze of orange juice), cover with foil and keep warm.

To grill the steak, preheat the grill to high and grill for about 4 minutes each side until it is brown on the outside but still pink inside. Turn off the grill and leave it to sit for a few minutes while you cook the spinach.

To roast the steak, heat the oven to 230°C/450°F/Gas Mark 8. Heat another tablespoon of oil in an ovenproof dish until it is very hot, then add the steak and brown quickly on all sides. Transfer to the oven and roast for 10–15 minutes. Remove, cover the dish and leave it to rest for a few minutes for the juices to sink back into the meat.

Cook the spinach according to the packet instructions. When it is done, drain well and stir through the walnut oil and walnuts. Slice the steak thinly before serving, and sprinkle the chopped chives and remaining orange zest over the beetroot.

To serve as a cold salad, simply replace the creamed spinach with a salad of baby spinach leaves with walnuts, dressed with balsamic vinegar and a mixture of walnut and good olive oil.

Calories:	335
Carbs:	7.19g
Protein:	18.44g
Fat:	26.06g
Saturated fat:	5.93g

Fish Dishes

Seafood Chowder

Fresh fish stock makes all the difference here – you can buy it in tubs in good super-markets, and it keeps well in the freezer. High-quality frozen seafood is also widely available now, but feel free to substitute any or all of this with fresh fish chunks.

   This is a super-tasty dish, and pretty enough to serve as a starter at a dinner party: you can make it a few hours in advance and then gently warm through before serving.

Serves 2

Preparation time: 10 minutes

Cooking time: 10 minutes

1 teaspoon olive oil

1 rasher bacon

1 medium onion, diced

1 medium carrot, peeled and diced

2 sticks celery, diced

275ml fish stock (or a tub of fish stock, made up to 275ml with water)

2 bay leaves

1 teaspoon fresh thyme leaves

1 strip lemon zest

100g seafood, or a mixture of seafood and fresh fish chunks

Black pepper

Lemon juice (optional)

1 tablespoon cream (optional)

In a heavy-based pan with a lid, fry the bacon in the olive oil until cooked. Add the onion and fry until soft. Add the carrot and celery and fry for a minute more. Add the fish stock, bay leaves, thyme and lemon zest, and bring to the boil. Add the seafood and simmer gently for 3 minutes, or until done. Taste for seasoning – a few grinds of black pepper might be nice, and add a squeeze of lemon juice before adding any salt.

Just before serving, stir in the cream.

Calories:	138
Carbs:	10.74g
Protein:	13.42g
Fat:	5.07g
Saturated fat:	0.65g

Roast Trout Fillets with Bacon and Green Beans

Trout is a wonderful fish for children as they seem to like both the texture and the not-very-fishy taste (it's better than salmon in this respect). Pairing it with bacon is also a winner.

Serves 4
Preparation time: 5 minutes
Cooking time: 10–15 minutes
4 rashers bacon
4 trout fillets (about 100g each)
400g green beans, topped and tailed
(300g new potatoes – for the children only!)

Preheat the oven to 180°C/350°F/Gas Mark 4 and place a baking tray in it to heat up. If you are doing potatoes for the children, put them on to boil now.

When the oven has heated up and the potatoes are boiling, slice the bacon thinly and fry it gently until well cooked, but not too crispy. Set aside on kitchen towel to drain the excess fat. Turn up the heat under the pan and, when it is hot enough, fry the trout fillets skin side down for 3 minutes. Remove them from the pan, place them on the preheated baking tray and put in the oven for 7–10 minutes, depending on their thickness. Return the pan to a gentle heat and keep the bacon warm in it while the trout finishes cooking.

Put a pan of water on to boil and add the green beans (though if the potatoes still need a few minutes I see no reason why you can't just tip the beans into the potato pot!).

Serve the trout with the beans on the side, and the bacon scattered over it.

	Without potatoes	With potatoes
Calories:	185	238
Carbs:	5.32g	17.39g
Protein:	22.58g	23.85g
Fat:	8.18g	8.40g
Saturated fat:	1.40g	1.40g

Grilled Tuna Steak with Gremolata and a Mixed Bean Salad

Fresh tuna is the 'steak' of the fish world, so if you are trying to cut down on your red meat this is a great alternative. It's simple to grill and can be flavoured in many different ways. Here I simply marinate it in lemon juice and pepper, and match it with a salad that is full of texture and flavour. You can use any type of olive – most deli counters now sell them stuffed with peppers, anchovies, lemon, garlic, almonds... I like them stuffed with chilli for this dish, to give a bit of extra bite. Marinated artichoke hearts add a very distinctive flavour. Look for them in the deli section and in jars in the supermarket.

   Gremolata is an Italian condiment made from very finely chopped parsley, lemon zest and garlic. You can sprinkle it over baked chicken legs or put the leftovers into a jam jar, cover it with olive oil and – hey presto – instant salad dressing!

Serves 2
Preparation time: 15 minutes
Cooking time: 10 minutes
1 juicy lemon
2 x 125g tuna steaks
Black pepper
1 can (410g) cannellini or haricot beans
50g pitted olives (see above)
3 whole marinated artichoke hearts (12 quarters)
1 teaspoon capers in brine
1 tablespoon extra virgin olive oil
2 tablespoons white wine vinegar
30g parsley
1 clove garlic
1 bag rocket

Cut the zest off the lemon using a zester or a potato peeler. Squeeze the juice of half the lemon over the tuna steaks, and add several grindings of black pepper. Set aside to marinate for up to half an hour.

Drain and rinse the beans and add them to the olives in a large mixing bowl (if the olives are large you may want to cut them in half). Chop the artichoke hearts into bite-size chunks, and chop the capers very finely. Add to the bowl with the olive oil and white wine vinegar, and mix everything together well.

To make the gremolata, cut the stalks off the parsley and then chop it very finely with the lemon zest and garlic. You can do this either with a very sharp knife, a herb cutter if you have one or a small blender (but take care you don't end up with a paste).

Set the grill to high, and grill the tuna for 5 minutes each side. While it is grilling, add the rocket leaves to the bean salad and toss gently to combine.

When the tuna is done, pile the salad on to each plate, place the tuna on the side and sprinkle the gremolata lightly over it.

Calories:	461
Carbs:	46.35g
Protein:	42.95g
Fat:	12.96g
Saturated fat:	2.01g

Thai-style Steamed Hake with Spinach and Gingered Carrots

A lovely light supper with Thai flavourings.

Serves 2
Preparation time: 15 minutes
Cooking time: 15 minutes

For the carrots:
1 teaspoon butter
½ teaspoon finely grated ginger
300g carrots, peeled and sliced
½ teaspoon sugar
Black pepper

For the fish:
Small bunch of spring onions
150g fillet of hake per person
2.5cm knob of ginger, grated
2 teaspoons sherry
2 teaspoons soy sauce

For the spinach:
455g spinach
1 dessertspoon olive oil
½ teaspoon freshly grated ginger

For the carrots
Melt the butter in a medium, lidded saucepan, add the grated ginger and carrots and stir to coat.

Add boiling water to half cover the carrots, add the sugar and pepper, put on the lid and allow to cook gently. The water should evaporate as the carrots cook. Shake occasionally and check that the carrots aren't burning. Depending on the age of the carrots, they will be cooked in 15–20 minutes. While they are cooking, put plates in the oven to warm, and prepare the fish.

For the fish

Trim the spring onions, slice vertically and lay on a plate that fits in your steamer. Rinse and dry the hake fillets and lay them on the spring onions. Add the ginger to the sherry and soy sauce and pour on to the fish.

Steam for 8–15 minutes: thin fillets will be done in 8 minutes; thicker ones may take up to 12. To check whether the fish is done, slip a knife between the flakes: if the flesh is opaque right through, the fish is cooked. While the fish is steaming, prepare the spinach.

For the spinach

455g of spinach collapses down to about half the amount when cooked, which is ample for two.

Wash the spinach thoroughly. Place in a saucepan with a tight-fitting lid and put on a low heat, shaking occasionally. The spinach should cook down in 5–10 minutes. Drain, pressing well through a colander or sieve, then slice. Drizzle with a little olive oil mixed with some finely grated ginger. Lay the spinach on the plates, with the hake on top of it and the carrots to one side.

Calories:	336
Carbs:	28.07g
Protein:	37.07g
Fat:	8.70g
Saturated fat:	2.73g

Carb Curfew Soups and Stews

Minestrone Soup

Real minestrone soup has to have a very dark-green vegetable, Parmesan cheese and bits of Parma ham floating in it. Forget those thin restaurant versions – this is the real thing. It's worth making for Saturday lunchtime, and finishing up the leftovers on Sunday evening.

Serves 2, with leftovers
Preparation time: 20 minutes
Cooking time: 20 minutes
2 tablespoons olive oil
3 slices streaky bacon or Parma ham, chopped
1 large onion, chopped
1 large carrot, chopped
2 sticks celery, chopped
3 cloves garlic, chopped finely
2 courgettes, cut into small cubes
200g green beans, cut into small chunks
300g dark-green cabbage, spring greens or curly kale, stems removed and leaves shredded finely
570ml light chicken or vegetable stock
2 cans (410g) cannellini beans
30g Parmesan cheese, grated
Salt and freshly ground black pepper

Heat the olive oil in a large, lidded, heavy-based pan and add the bacon or Parma ham. Cook until crisp, then remove and set aside to drain on kitchen paper. In the remaining oil, fry the onion and cook till translucent. Add the chopped carrot, celery and garlic and cook for a further few minutes until the carrot softens. Add the courgettes, green beans, cabbage, chicken stock and one of the cans of cannellini beans, put the lid on and simmer for 20 minutes, checking after 10 minutes to make sure it's not sticking (add a cup of water if it is).

When the soup is done, take a ladleful of the liquid and whiz it with the second can of beans and half the Parmesan to make a thick liquid. Return this to the pot, stir and heat through till just simmering. Season to taste, but add Parmesan before any salt.

Serve in large bowls and sprinkle the remaining Parmesan on top.

Calories:	469
Carbs:	45.81g
Protein:	27.89g
Fat:	33.70g
Saturated fat:	6.09g

Chicken Soup

A good chicken stock is the perfect base for a large variety of substantial soups, and gently poached chicken is delicious, low-fat and versatile. A free-range and preferably organic chicken is best for this dish. A whole chicken is cheaper than ready-jointed portions.

Makes enough for 4 people
1 chicken, rinsed inside and out in several changes of water
1 onion (skin on), quartered
1 carrot
6 peppercorns
1 bay leaf

To poach the chicken
Place the chicken in a heavy-based, lidded saucepan with the other ingredients and cover with water. Bring to simmering point, and simmer, covered, for 45 minutes, skimming off any scum which floats to the surface from time to time. Test for doneness by lifting from the poaching liquid and poking the thigh with a knife to make sure that the juices run clear. Allow to cool in the stock, and refrigerate once cool.

To strip the carcass
Transfer the chicken to a large plate or a chopping board with a groove around the edges to catch the juices. Remove the meat and discard all skin and fat. Return the bones to the stock and cook for a further half hour to extract all the flavour. Throw out the bones and cool the stock. The chicken meat will keep perfectly fresh and moist refrigerated in the stock for a couple of days. Now you have your stock and your meat, there are a number of options: Thai, Italian or French.

Italian-style Chicken Soup

Serves 4

3 cloves garlic, sliced

3 medium courgettes, cut in half and sliced

1 teaspoon olive oil

1 litre chicken stock

Sprig rosemary

400g chicken meat

1 tin (410g) chickpeas

15g flat-leaf parsley, finely chopped

1 teaspoon chilli oil (optional)

15g grated Parmesan cheese (optional)

Cook the garlic and courgettes gently in the oil, then add the chicken stock and rosemary. Bring to simmering point, then add the chicken meat and chickpeas. Warm through, remove the rosemary and serve in shallow bowls with the parsley. Season with chilli oil and/or Parmesan, if desired.

Calories:	325
Carbs:	26.29g
Protein:	37.87g
Fat:	6.90g
Saturated fat:	1.47g

Thai-style Chicken Soup

It really is worth using fresh ingredients for this soup, but if you're in a hurry then by all means use puréed versions of the lemon grass, garlic and ginger; and you can substitute 2 teaspoons of Thai green curry paste for the turmeric/coriander/cumin spice mix. Thai fish sauce comes in tiny bottles which keep well, and it's great for adding authentic flavour to Asian foods.

Serves 4

3 sticks lemon grass, bruised and with outer leaves removed (or 1 teaspoon lemon
 grass purée)

1 knob ginger, peeled (or 1 teaspoon ginger purée)

3 cloves garlic (or 1½ teaspoons garlic purée)

1 small onion, diced

2 teaspoons turmeric

1 teaspoon coriander

1 teaspoon cumin

½ teaspoon cayenne pepper (optional)

1 tablespoon sunflower oil

1 litre chicken stock

1 tin (400ml) reduced-fat coconut milk

400g chicken meat

30g fresh coriander, chopped

6 spring onions, sliced

½ teaspoon Nam Pla fish sauce (optional)

1 juicy lime (optional)

If you are using fresh spices, then finely mince the lemon grass, ginger, garlic, onion and other spices in a food processor. Otherwise, simply mix the different puréed spices and pastes with the diced onion in a small bowl. Cook this spicy blend in the oil until aromatic, then add the chicken stock and bring to simmering point.

Add the coconut milk and the chicken meat and warm through, then add the coriander and spring onions and serve in large bowls. Season with fish sauce and lime juice, if desired.

Calories:	316
Carbs:	8.89g
Protein:	34.04g
Fat:	15.32g
Saturated fat:	6.28g

French-style Chicken Soup

Serves 4

1 litre chicken stock

15g tarragon, chopped

12 baby leeks, trimmed and chopped

12 baby carrots, trimmed and chopped

2 bulbs fennel, cores removed and chopped

400g chicken meat

1 bunch flat-leaf parsley, chopped

Bring the stock to simmering point with the tarragon and vegetables. Simmer until the vegetables are cooked, then add the chicken meat and heat through. Serve with the parsley sprinkled over the top.

Calories:	205
Carbs:	7.32g
Protein:	32.99g
Fat:	4.22g
Saturated fat:	1.15g

Vegetable Stew

This quick vegetable stew is simple, cleansing and comforting. It can be prepared with store cupboard ingredients and whatever's in the vegetable drawer. Quantities given are for two – it's easy to double or treble as required but don't try to freeze the leftovers as root vegetables become unpleasantly fuzzy when frozen. For the stock, a low-salt vegetable or chicken stock cube is fine; but if you have a carcass left from a roast chicken, boil that up with some onion, carrot, celery and peppercorns to make your own.

Serves 2

Preparation time: 10 minutes

Cooking time: 15 minutes

1 tablespoon olive oil

2 cloves garlic, sliced into 2 or 3

2 leeks, sliced into 2.5cm lengths

2 carrots, sliced into 2.5cm lengths

2 small or 1 medium courgette, sliced into 2.5cm lengths

285ml stock

Bunch thyme and a bay leaf

1 tin Puy lentils, drained and rinsed (175g drained weight)

Freshly ground black pepper

1 dessertspoon liquid from preserved lemons (optional: see note)

1 good bunch parsley, finely chopped

Heat the olive oil. Add the garlic, leeks and carrots and stir well to coat with the oil. Cover and leave to cook on a gentle heat for 5 minutes.

Add the courgettes, cover and leave for another 5 minutes. Then add the stock, thyme and bay leaf, and allow to simmer until the carrot chunks are tender. Add the lentils and a good grinding of black pepper, and warm through.

Remove the bay leaf and thyme, serve in soup bowls with the parsley on top, and stir in the liquid from the preserved lemons if desired.

Note: You can buy preserved lemons in many supermarkets now. If you want to make your own then wash organic lemons, cut into thin-ish slices and pack into jars with good handfuls of sea salt and generous squeezes of lemon juice. Press down to ensure that the lemon slices are covered with liquid. Cover top of jars with olive oil. Leave in a cool, dark place for two to three weeks. Use as a condiment.

Calories:	237
Carbs:	33.56g
Protein:	10.86g
Fat:	7.73g
Saturated fat:	1.09g

Hotpot with Haricot or Cannellini Beans

This is a lovely, warming, easy-to-prepare dish. You can ring the changes by adding other vegetables according to season. If you prepare it a day in advance, you can skim off any fat before reheating. Advance preparation also gives the flavours time to mellow and the lamb to become meltingly tender.

Serves 4

Preparation time: 15 minutes

Cooking time: 1½ hours

2 tablespoons olive oil

1kg shoulder or neck of lamb, trimmed of fat and cut into chunks

12 baby carrots, cleaned

12 baby leeks, cleaned

750ml stock (vegetable, chicken or lamb)

1 sprig thyme

1 tin haricot or cannellini beans

Freshly ground black pepper

1 tablespoon parsley, freshly chopped

Heat the oil in a large, lidded casserole dish, and brown the cubes of lamb, in batches if necessary. Remove it from the pan to a plate, and then use the residual oil to brown the carrots and leeks.

Heat the stock. Layer the meat and vegetables in the casserole dish, add the stock and thyme, and bring to the boil on the stove top. Put on the lid and place in a medium oven. Check occasionally – if the hotpot looks dry, top up with a little water.

After an hour, drain and rinse the tinned beans, and stir them into the hot-pot. Return the casserole to the oven for a further 15–20 minutes. Season to taste and top with the chopped parsley.

Calories:	443
Carbs:	19.60g
Protein:	26.8g
Fat:	28.26g
Saturated fat:	11.06g

Winter Vegetable Soup or Bake

This soup base can very easily be turned into a baked dish simply by using a little less stock, and serving it with a crusty cheese topping. You could make double quantities of the basic mix and freeze half so you have a delicious soup one day, with the leftovers giving you a quick and easy base for a warming baked supper. You don't have to stick to this mixture of vegetables, but butternut squash does give a lovely sweet flavour, which goes surprisingly well with the mushrooms.

The secret is not to boil green vegetables to death – they lose vitamins and colour if you do.

Serves 2
Preparation time: 15 minutes
Cooking time: 15 minutes (soup), 35 minutes (bake)

1 medium onion, chopped finely

2 medium carrots, peeled and chopped

200g mixed mushrooms, wiped and quartered

2 sticks celery, sliced thickly

1 tablespoon olive oil

2 cloves garlic, mashed

½ a medium butternut squash, peeled and cubed

1 medium parsnip, peeled and cubed

500ml vegetable stock

1 bouquet garni

1 can (410g) borlotti, cannellini or haricot beans

2 medium leeks, washed and sliced

¼ medium Savoy cabbage, washed and thinly sliced

For the bake only

100g low-fat Cheddar cheese, grated

100g French beans, trimmed

In a heavy-based saucepan, gently cook the onion, carrots, mushrooms and celery in the olive oil till soft, then add the garlic and cook for a minute more. Add the squash cubes, parsnip and stock, and stir gently till mixed together. Add the bouquet garni and simmer gently with the lid on for about 15 minutes until the vegetables are soft but still retain a little bite. You may need to add a little water to stop it sticking. When they are done, transfer about a third of the vegetables to a small bowl, and mash them roughly with a fork – this will be used to thicken the soup. Set aside for a few minutes.

Add the beans, leeks and cabbage, stir gently and cook with the lid on for another 5 or so minutes until the beans are warmed through and the cabbage and leeks are soft. Remove the bouquet garni, return half of the mashed soup mix to the pot, and stir gently until it has all thickened. Add more mashed soup if you prefer your soup thick and a little water if it needs thinning down. Discard any remaining mashed vegetables.

You can eat the soup like this, but if you would prefer to make it into a more substantial supper, then be sparing with the stock in the first stages of the dish and add all of the mashed vegetables to the pot to thicken it. Stir it all in (gently, as you don't want to break up the squash pieces) and then pour this thick soup base into a shallow pie dish. Sprinkle the Cheddar over the top and bake in a preheated oven (180°C/350°F/Gas Mark 4) for about 25 minutes until the cheese is bubbling. While it is baking, microwave the beans in a clingfilmed bowl for 3 minutes, drain and then serve.

	Not baked	Baked
Calories:	386	485
Carbs:	61.35g	65.16g
Protein:	21.28g	34.18g
Fat:	8.48g	12.03g
Saturated fat:	1.14g	3.32g

Carb Curfew Desserts

When following Carb Curfew, it's important to cut out potatoes, bread, rice and pasta from your evening meal. Sugar and flour, which can be found in some of the following recipes, are not so much of an issue.

Low-fat New York Lemon Cheesecake with Raspberries

This baked cheesecake has a light lemon flavour that goes fabulously well with any sort of soft fruit, but particularly raspberries. It's made with Quark, a very low-fat cheese, which you can find in health-food shops and some supermarkets. If you can't find fresh raspberries, then you can make a hot sauce with frozen berries.

Serves 8
Preparation time: 20 minutes
Cooking time: 1 hour (depending on the size of your cake tin)
Zest and juice of 1 lemon
1 teaspoon vanilla extract
120g caster sugar
500g Quark
4 egg whites
90g self-raising flour
500g fresh raspberries (or frozen berries: see above)
1–2 teaspoons caster sugar (optional)

You will need either an 18cm or 20cm tin for this – preferably a spring-form tin that can be opened at the side. Alternatively, use a regular (deep-sided) cake tin, but oil it a little first and then line it well with greaseproof paper.

Preheat the oven to 190°C/375°F/Gas Mark 5.

Put the lemon juice and vanilla in a small bowl, and add the sugar, stirring until it dissolves. Set aside. In a large mixing bowl, stir the Quark with a wooden spoon until creamy, then add the lemon/vanilla/sugar mixture and stir well again.

With a clean hand-held mixer, take another (clean) mixing bowl and whip the egg whites until they form soft peaks. Pour the self-raising flour into the Quark mixture and beat well with the electric mixer until it is all incorporated – you may have to scrape down the sides of the bowl here.

Tip a third of the egg whites into the Quark mixture and stir with a wooden spoon to lighten the mix. Then add the rest of the egg whites and fold in gently, getting right into the corners of the bowl, and tip it gently into the prepared tin.

Place it in the middle of the oven and cook for an hour *without opening the door* or the cake will sink. When an hour is up, remove it from the oven and place on a rack to cool for 15 minutes.

While it is cooling, take half of the raspberries and push them through a sieve to make a coulis. If you have frozen berries, bring them to a gentle simmer in a heavy-based saucepan and cook for a few minutes until they begin to soften. Taste the berries and add a little sugar if necessary.

To serve, unmould the cheesecake and cut into wedges. Serve with a drizzle of coulis and a few berries.

Calories:	187
Carbs:	33.97g
Protein:	12.40g
Fat:	0.51g
Saturated fat:	0.03g

Mixed Berry Salad with Low-fat Creamy Dressing

As a low-fat alternative to cream, this can't be beaten. Tofu, despite its hippy connotations, is a wonderful protein source, and low in cholesterol and fat. It has hardly any taste, but if you whiz it up in a blender with some of the berries you capture its creaminess and give it a berry taste. You can buy it in Tetra Paks in the health-food section of most supermarkets: look for 'silken style', which is smoother in texture.

Fresh berries are wonderfully good for you, and a combination of blueberries, raspberries and strawberries not only looks great, but gives you a delightful purple cream too. You can prepare everything in advance (which makes it a lovely end to a dinner party) and serve in glass bowls or large wine glasses for the full effect. If you can't find fresh berries, then simply simmer a bag of frozen berries for about five minutes, leave to cool, and use that instead. Take out the frozen strawberries, though – they are horrid when cooked.

Serves 2
Preparation time: 10 minutes
100g soft tofu, drained of any excess packaging water
100g blueberries
100g raspberries
200g strawberries (though see note about frozen fruit above)
4 teaspoons honey or maple syrup
Orange or lemon juice (optional)
2 sprigs fresh mint (optional)

Drain the tofu of excess water by cutting a hole in the packaging, laying it on its side on the draining board, and then placing a couple of plates on top to squeeze the water out.

Take a few of each of the berries, and whiz up in a blender with the drained tofu and the honey or maple syrup. Check the taste: you might like to add a squeeze of orange or lemon juice.

Layer the low-fat cream with the berries in glass bowls, and garnish with a sprig of mint.

Calories:	189
Carbs:	33.45g
Protein:	7.89g
Fat:	4.24g
Saturated fat:	0.55g

Banana Muffins

This dessert also makes a great weekend brunch. Two muffins, a little sugar-free fruit jam, a glass of prune juice and herbal tea adds up to just 400 calories.

Serves 6 (makes 12 muffins)
Preparation time: 15 minutes
Cooking time: 25 minutes
200g unbleached white flour
½ teaspoon bicarbonate of soda
1 teaspoon baking powder
½ teaspoon ground cinnamon
¼ teaspoon nutmeg
60g brown sugar
100g porridge oats
1 egg white
1 egg
2 tablespoons sunflower oil
2 ripe bananas, mashed
50g low-fat natural yoghurt
50g sultanas

Preheat the oven to 200°C/400°F/Gas Mark 6. Prepare a muffin tin with paper liners, cooking spray or a fine coating of oil.

Sift together the flour, bicarbonate, baking powder and spices and stir in the sugar. Process the oats in a blender and stir into the other dry ingredients. Beat the egg white for 3 minutes until increased in volume but not stiff. Stir in the egg, oil, bananas, yoghurt and sultanas. Fold the wet ingredients into the dry until just combined but not too homogeneous.

Spoon the batter into the muffin tin, and bake for 20–25 minutes until a skewer comes out clean (a length of spaghetti works just as well for this!). Allow to cool in the tin for 5 minutes, then transfer to a cooling rack.

Per serving (2 muffins)	
Calories:	150
Protein:	5.1g
Carbs:	31.0g
Fat:	3.4g
Saturated fat:	0g

Cinnamon-poached Fruit

This works well as a cold dessert, but is also great in the morning with a dollop of low-fat yoghurt. It keeps for days in the fridge if you cover it with clingfilm. Choose your own combination of fruit, or buy 'dried fruit salad' from the health-food shop.

Serves 6

Preparation time: 5 minutes
Cooking time: 40 minutes
250g mixed dried apple, apricot, pineapple, prune, mango, cherry, blueberry
2 cinnamon sticks
4 tablespoons honey

Place the dried fruit in a large heavy-based casserole dish with the cinnamon sticks and honey. Pour in water to cover by at least 2.5cm and simmer gently for 40 minutes, checking fairly frequently to make sure that the water hasn't evaporated: you want to be able to serve this with a good amount of delicious juice.

When the fruit have plumped and softened, remove from the heat, leave to cool and then refrigerate. This dish benefits from being made the day before to allow the flavours to develop. Depending on your choice of fruit, you may want to add a little more honey before serving.

Calories:	144
Carbs:	38.23g
Protein:	1.07g
Fat:	0.21g
Saturated fat:	Trace

Snacks

All these snacks contain no more than 200 calories.

- 1 small pot natural, low-fat bio yoghurt, on its own or mixed with 2 tablespoons dried fruit and 1 teaspoon honey
- 2 brazil nuts
- 3 dried figs
- 30g almonds (about 24 nuts)
- 1 whole-wheat cracker such as Ryvita spread with avocado
- 3 whole-wheat crackers such as Ryvita each topped with 1 teaspoon fat-free cream cheese and 1 teaspoon mango chutney
- Fruity Burrito: 2 tablespoons fat-free cream cheese and 2 teaspoons all-fruit sugar-free jam spread on a heated 20cm flour tortilla filled with ½ sliced banana and rolled up.
- 1 slice date and walnut bread
- 1 small glass skimmed milk
- 1 slice Low-fat New York Lemon Cheesecake with Raspberries (see page 296)
- 1 handful chopped baby carrots
- 1 matchbox-size piece of Cheddar cheese and a Granny Smith apple
- 1 cup blueberries and raspberries topped with a tablespoon of low-fat bio yoghurt and 3 chopped walnuts
- 1 baked apple stuffed with ½ teaspoon ground cinnamon and 2 teaspoons brown sugar
- ½ whole-wheat bagel, toasted and topped with 2 teaspoons all-fruit sugar-free apricot jam and a cup of Earl Grey tea

Glossary

Adipocytes: Fat cells found under the skin and around the delicate organs of the body.

Adipose tissue: Connective tissue made up of fat cells. Found directly under the skin and around the delicate organs of the body to provide protection.

Adrenal gland: Orange coloured endocrine glands, located on the top of both kidneys. They produce a number of hormones, specifically epinephrine and norepinephrine (adrenaline), the hormones released during stress and exercise.

Aerobic capacity: The body's ability to consume oxygen at a cell level and produce energy.

Atrophic gastritis: A bacterial infection marked by a decreased ability to produce sufficient amounts of gastric acids.

Blood pressure: The pressure exerted by the blood on the walls of the arteries, measured in millimetres of mercury by the sphygmomanometer.

Body mass index (BMI): A relative measure of body height to body weight for determining degree of obesity.

Break-point walking: A pace where you are walking so fast you are just about to break into a jog. While I don't recommend you walk at your break point for long periods, it is useful to help you find your optimum walking pace.

Calorie or kilocalorie (kcal): The amount of heat energy needed to raise the temperature of 1 kilogram of water by 1°C, commonly used as a measure of energy in food.

Carb Curfew: No bread, pasta, rice, potatoes or cereal after 5pm. It is a useful strategy that helps you get the right balance of calories and nutrients at the right time of day.

Carbohydrates (simple and complex): An essential nutrient that provides energy to the body. Dietary sources include sugars (simple) and grains, rice, potatoes and beans (complex). 1g carbohydrate = 4 kcal.

Cardiovascular exercise (cardio): Moving your body with the use of the large muscle groups. Uses oxygen as a source of energy, and strengthens the heart, lungs and circulatory system.

Cellulite: A non-medical term often used to describe subcutaneous fat, commonly found in the thighs and buttocks, which appears dimpled like orange peel. Nutritional authorities agree that all forms of subcutaneous fat are the same and that cellulite is not a special form of fat.

Cholesterol: A fatty substance found in the blood and body tissues and in animal products, essential for the production of hormones and steroids. Its accumulation in the arteries leads to narrowing of the arteries (atherosclerosis).

Cortisol: The most important hormone to training and conditioning. Cortisol is a primary signal hormone for carbohydrate metabolism and is related to the glycogen stores in the muscles.

Diabetes: A disease of carbohydrate metabolism in which an absolute or relative deficiency of insulin results in an inability to metabolize carbohydrates normally.

Epinephrine: A hormone produced by the adrenal glands, important for preparing the body for an emergency. Often referred to as the 'fight or flight' hormone, it also has an important role to play in helping the body break down fat.

Exercise Intensity: The physiological stress on the body during exercise. Indicates how hard the body should be working to achieve a training effect.

Fats (saturated, polyunsaturated, monounsaturated, trans/hydrogenated): An essential nutrient that provides energy, energy storage and insulation to the body. 1g fat = 9 kcal.

Fibre: Dietary fibre is mainly derived from plant cell walls. There are two types of dietary fibre: soluble and insoluble.

Glucose: A simple sugar; the form in which all carbohydrates are used as the body's principal energy source.

Glycaemic Index (GI): Classifies a food according to the degree to which it raises blood glucose. The reference foods are glucose or white bread, which are given a rating of 100.

Glycaemic Load (GL): Takes serving sizes into account, unlike the GI. To calculate the GL of a food, multiply the grams of carbohydrate in the food by the serving size in grams divided by 100. Consuming a lot of a high-GI food will bring about a greater glycaemic response than eating a small amount of a high-GI food.

Glycogen: The storage form of glucose found in the liver and muscles.

Growth hormone: A hormone produced by the pituitary gland, released into the bloodstream in far greater quantities when we are young, peaking in our mid-20s and then beginning a gradual decline. Responsible for growth and efficient cell functioning.

High-density lipoproteins (HDLs): A microscopic complex of specialized fats called lipids and proteins. HDLs contain relatively more protein and less cholesterol and triglycerides than low-density lipoproteins (see entry). High HDL levels are associated with a lower risk of coronary heart disease.

Hormones: Chemical messengers that are synthesized, stored and released into the blood by endocrine glands.

Hyperglycaemia: An abnormally high content of glucose in the blood.

Hypertension: High blood pressure or the elevation of blood pressure above 140/90mmHg.

Hypoglycaemia: A deficiency of sugar in the blood, commonly caused by too much insulin.

Hypothalamus: Section of the brain primarily responsible for linking the communication of the brain with the body.

Insulin: A hormone secreted by the pancreas. Helps the body utilize blood glucose (blood sugar) by binding with receptors on cells like a key would fit into a lock. Once the key – insulin – has unlocked the door, the glucose can pass from the blood into the cell. Inside the cell, glucose is either used for energy or stored for future use in the form of glycogen in liver or muscle cells.

Insulin resistance: Occurs when the normal amount of insulin secreted by the pancreas is not able to unlock the door to cells. To maintain normal blood glucose, the pancreas secretes additional insulin. In some cases (about a third of people with insulin resistance), when the body cells resist or do not respond to even higher levels of insulin, glucose builds up in the blood, leading to high blood glucose or type 2 diabetes.

Interval training: Short, high-intensity exercise periods alternated with periods of rest or less intensive active recovery. Example: 100-metre brisk walk, 1-minute moderate-paced walk, repeated eight times.

Lipolysis: Technical term for the breakdown of fat.

Low-density lipoproteins (LDLs): A microscopic complex of lipids and proteins that contains relatively more cholesterol and triglycerides and less protein than high-density lipoproteins (see entry). High LDL levels are associated with an increased risk of coronary heart disease.

Menopause: Cessation of menstruation in the human female, usually occurring between the ages of 48 and 50.

Metabolism: The chemical and physiological processes in the body that provide energy for the maintenance of life.

Muscle mass (or fat-free mass): Composed of bone, muscle and organs.

Neutral position: Thought to be the best position for good posture. The lumbar spine and pelvis should not be flexed, extended, tilted or rotated.

Nutrients (and micronutrients): Life-sustaining substances found in food. They work together to supply the body with energy and structural materials and to regulate growth, maintenance and repair of the body's tissues.

Oestrogen: One of the female hormones that helps regulate a woman's passage through menstruation, fertility and menopause. One of the most powerful hormones in the human body.

Omega-3 fatty acids: A form of blood fat, found mainly in oily fish and flax and pumpkin seeds.

Optimum walking pace: The correct walking pace to establish improvements in your fitness and achieve weight loss, 3–5 per cent slower than your break point (see entry).

Pedometer: A simple device you attach to your belt. It records each step through a sensory device registering motion at the hip.

Perceived exertion rate: Method used to regulate intensity during aerobic endurance training. Rating is recorded numerically by your own perception of how hard you are working.

Peri-menopause: The stage leading up to full menopause in a woman's life cycle. This can be up to eight years before full menopause.

Portion distortion: An inaccurate serving size of different foods.

Probiotic: Micro-organisms used in a positive way to benefit health. Usually consumed in specially designed 'functional' foods, probiotics are commonly ingested as bacteria in live yoghurt to enhance the intestinal flora and so aid digestion.

Resistance exercise: Exerting a force to enable you to move or apply tension to a weight. Results in enhanced muscular strength.

Resting metabolic rate: The number of calories expended per unit of time at rest. It is measured early in the morning after an overnight fast and at least eight hours of sleep.

Rib-hip connection: Helps with abdominal contraction before lifting and ensures the correct anatomical position of the spine.

Strength training: See resistance exercise.

Structured exercise: Involves putting on your trainers, setting aside specific time to take exercise and getting a little bit hot and sweaty.

Testosterone: A male sex hormone, although women have testosterone levels one-tenth to one-twelfth those of men. Testosterone is the main hormone produced in the testicles.

Thermic effect of food: The increase in energy expenditure above the resting metabolic rate as a result of eating a meal.

Thermic effect of exercise: The energy expended in physical activity.

Weight-bearing exercise: Tones and uses your own body weight, such as Pilates, yoga and the strength exercises in your six-week plan.

Joanna Hall's 'Walk off Weight' Workout and Workshops

Now everyone has the chance to get personal advice from the UK's leading health and fitness expert

Whether your aim is to walk off weight, improve health or increase fitness, Joanna's sessions are devised to teach you how to get the most from walking, by giving you a personal prescription for success. Each workout and workshop will include a lecture on how to walk more effectively, lessons on how to use a pedometer correctly and a practical walking session led by Joanna.

For further information on where and when these 'Walk off Weight' workouts and workshops take place, check out www.joannahall.com.

Track your health with Joanna's Small Steps, Big Changes pedometer range

Joanna Hall's Small Steps, Big Changes pedometer range, developed with Walk4Life, carries the Gold Standard for research and is accurate and simple to use. There are two models, one measuring your steps and one measuring steps and time.

You can order these pedometers from Joanna's website at www.joannahall.com.